THE ART

The word 'ritual' is enough to frighten people off if they immediately conjure up images of a full-blown Golden Dawn affair with all the trappings of high drama. In *The Art of Ritual*, Rachel Patterson has stripped away all the myth and reduced ritual down to its lowest common denominator – simple and effective.

As someone whose magical training has been at both ends of the scale – from the formal, intense rituals of the Egyptian Mysteries to the informal, spontaneous elements of traditional British Old Craft – it was refreshing to read a book that covers the middle ground in a sensible and highly informative manner. An idle introduction to the practice of ritualised magic.
Mélusine Draco, Coven of the Scales

This is a really useful reference book for anyone who is wanting to create their own pagan rituals. The first part explains all the terminology and techniques you need to know, while the second part is full of ready-to-run examples. These include rites of passage such as hand fastings and baby namings, Wheel of the Year rites, Celtic tree celebrations, elemental rituals and rites to honour various Goddesses.
Lucya Starza, author of *Pagan Portals: Candle Magic*

The Art of
Ritual

The Art of
Ritual

Rachel Patterson

Winchester, UK
Washington, USA

First published by Moon Books, 2016
Moon Books is an imprint of John Hunt Publishing Ltd., Laurel House, Station Approach,
Alresford, Hants, SO24 9JH, UK
office1@jhpbooks.net
www.johnhuntpublishing.com
www.moon-books.net

For distributor details and how to order please visit the 'Ordering' section on our website.

ISBN: 978 1 78279 776 0
Library of Congress Control Number: 2015953412

A CIP catalogue record for this book is available from the British Library.

Design: Stuart Davies

Printed and bound by CPI Group (UK) Ltd, Croydon, CR0 4YY, UK

We operate a distinctive and ethical publishing philosophy in all
areas of our business, from our global network of authors to
production and worldwide distribution.

CONTENTS

Huge thanks to my husband Peter Patterson for designing the book cover and to my lovely friends who contributed ritual scripts, support and general insults; Tracey Roberts, Vanessa Armstrong, Samantha Leaver, Sue Perryman, Joshua Petchey and Stacey Mantle.

Who am I?

I am a witch...have been for a very long time, not the green skinned warty kind obviously...the real sort, but I am also a working wife and mother who has also been lucky enough to write and have published a book or three. I love to learn, I love to study and have done so from books, online resources, schools and wonderful mentors over the years and still continue to learn each and every day, but have learnt the most from actually getting outside and doing it.

I like to laugh...and eat cake...

Bibliography

Pagan Portals: Kitchen Witchcraft
Grimoire of a Kitchen Witch
Pagan Portals: Hoodoo Folk Magic
Pagan Portals: Moon Magic
A Kitchen Witch's World of Magical Plants & Herbs
A Kitchen Witch's World of Magical Foods
Pagan Portals: Meditation

Websites and social media

My website: www.rachelpatterson.co.uk
Facebook: www.facebook.com/rachelpattersonbooks
My personal blog: www.tansyfiredragon.blogspot.co.uk
Email: tansyfiredragon@yahoo.com
www.kitchenwitchhearth.net
www.kitchenwitchuk.blogspot.co.uk
www.facebook.com/kitchenwitchuk
www.thekitchenwitchcauldron.blogspot.co.uk

Kitchen Witch Coven

I am High Priestess of the Kitchen Witch Coven and an Elder at the online Kitchen Witch School of Natural Witchcraft.

My craft is a combination of old religion witchcraft, Wicca, kitchen witchery, hedge witchery and folk magic. My heart is that of a Kitchen Witch. I am blessed with a wonderful husband, lovely children, a fabulous family and good friends.

Ritual – What is It?

Don't be scared off by the word 'ritual' – all it means is a set of actions that come together to make a whole.

Rituals are performed by groups, but also by solitaries. Rituals can be as simple as daily actions you do to connect with deity right up to ceremonial circles and, of course, everything in between. We all do our own personal rituals every day; even simple rituals such as getting up, cleaning our teeth, showering and having breakfast. It is a set of actions that you put in motion.

I will take you through the basic format for a ritual, but you can add your own spin, make it simpler, make it more detailed – the choice is yours.

My personal inclination is to have a very relaxed ritual using the bare essentials, which obviously includes cake…and to have a little bit of laughter and frivolity in circle because, after all, the Gods have a sense of humour too. However, my basic training was in Wicca, which is much more structured, and I have also had druidic training and led several druid rituals as well, although my pathway now is that of a Kitchen/Hedge Witch so I can hopefully share all of my experiences and methods with you along with a broader spectrum of ideas. My advice is to take what works for you and make it your own. Have a bit of a pick-and-mix attitude and create something that is unique.

Visualisation

I think for any ritual to work well you need to be able to visualise. For instance, with the circle casting it really helps if you can 'see' the protective shield form around you. Good visualisation comes with practise. A basic exercise you can work with is to sit quietly with your eyes closed almost in a meditative state and visualise a piece of fruit, an apple works well. See the apple in your mind's eye; note the colour, the texture, and any imperfections to the skin. Visualise the apple turning around so that you can see all of it. Once you have this part of the exercise well practised move on to visualizing taking a bite of the apple, how it tastes and smells. Some people will have good skills in this area; others may just be able to feel the energy of the circle.

Energy Work

There is energy in all living things and by living I also include items such as shells and pebbles along with the more obvious plants, trees and humans. Each natural item has an energy field and you can, with practise, pick up the energy field and even tap into it. We do it with Mother Nature when we ground and we do it with the elements in ritual. When you invite an element to join you by calling in a quarter it works so much better if you can actually feel that element join you. When you are raising energy for spell work, again it will be easier and more manageable to be able to feel that energy. Your experience in ritual will be so much greater if you know how to work with or at least feel the energy that is raised.

One of the first exercises we always ask anyone to work with when they start on this pathway is to feel energy. Sit or stand, where you are right now will be fine. Then rub your hands together quickly for a few seconds then very slowly pull them a few inches apart then gently push them back together. Do you feel a resistance? If you do then this is the energy that we need to work with. Once you are an old hand (no pun intended) at energy work you should be able to feel a person's energy when they are a few feet away from you.

Part 1

Ritual Basics

Tools of the Trade

I just want to emphasise here...you don't need any fancy tools to hold a ritual, in fact you don't need any tools at all. However, I will give a list of the items commonly used in case you want to try the ceremonial route, it is a very personal choice. Sometimes it is nice to go the whole hog and put on a big ceremony with all the bells and whistles, but it is also good to just have an impromptu ritual in the middle of a field with nothing but some pebbles and sticks. You are the power; the magic is within you so tools aren't necessary. Having said that tools can carry their own power; each tool has an element that it corresponds with and they can be consecrated and charged with energy as well and they can give us a focus to work with, it really is your call. If you haven't worked with tools before my suggestion would be experiment, see what works for you. I have often found that handmade tools work better than machine/mass-produced ones, especially if you make them yourself, because you add your own energy into them.

The power and energy you receive from a tool will also depend on what material it is made from along with any specific designs or symbols it has on it. A copper wand will react differently to one made from oak for instance, add a quartz crystal to the end and the energy will take on another dimension again.

Part of this journey when working with tools of any sort is to fathom out which ones work in harmony with each other and for what specific intent or magical purpose. Again, this is personal, what works for one person may not work well for another.

Altar

A lot of pagans will have an altar (or in my case and much to my husband's dismay, several altars) set up at home. If you hold your ritual in the room you have your usual altar set up in then you are part way there already.

Your altar is many things, not just a place to hold your magical tools, but also somewhere you can sit and meditate in front of, use as a focal point for spell work and also as a place to honour the seasons and deity. It is a mini sacred space and a place that over time will soak up the magical energies when you work with the tools on it and when you spellcast around it. It is a place for you to 'touch base' with deity, the divine and your inner magical self on a daily basis. For instance, I have a working altar, this one I decorate for the energies of each month, but I also have another altar dedicated to my matron and patron deities; then I have a kitchen altar, one in the garden for the Fae and also one in my office for things I am currently working with. Each one is different and has its own very individual style and energy.

When we hold our coven rituals we have a very practical altar; it has to be transported through the woods so it starts out in the car as a large plastic box which holds all the bits for the ritual. When we get to our grove of trees we empty it and turn it upside down, then it is covered with a pretty, silk altar cloth. Our portable altar is then ready to hold the items we need for the ritual, which usually consists of a cauldron for the incense, chalice for the drink, flower petals to cast the circle, our script books and occasionally a seasonal decoration. We are in the middle of a forest having had to walk some way from the cars carrying not only the altar, but also flasks of drink, cups, ritual items and of course plenty of cake boxes, so we keep the altar simple.

However, for a ritual altar at home it is much easier to add whatever items you want and as many as you want.

I do think it pertinent to mention here…clean your altar regularly, it gathers dust very quickly and that can cause blockages in energy flow.

If you are not 'out of the broom closet' at home or sharing a house with others who wouldn't appreciate you setting up altars all over the house, it can be done in several ways. Keep all your altar items on a tray in a cupboard then just bring the tray out when you need to use it or have your altar inside a cupboard so you can close the doors to it when necessary or have your altar on a shelf. If you are really being a secret squirrel then just a shelf or windowsill with a candle and a vase of flowers works perfectly well as a basic altar, no one would ever know.

Traditionally (and by that I really mean more along the Wiccan lines) your altar will hold specific items; representations of the four elements, deity (the God, the Goddess, the divine); often it will hold a pentacle in some form and then items that you are working with.

Here are the main items, this list is not comprehensive nor do you need to rush out and purchase all of the items (your altar would be pretty crowded with every item on the list on it). In fact, some items you may never use, I boringly repeat…it is personal, go with what works for you. When I first started on this pathway I made out a list of all the things I 'needed' and did a whole big shopping trip which, apart from being hugely out of pocket, resulted in me having items that I have never once used and a lot that now sit in the cupboard gathering dust. I have two beautiful athames, which I have not used, preferring to cast a circle with my finger. I have four gorgeous wooden wands, all made from sacred woods and hand carved which, while they often sit on my altar, I don't actually use. I have two chalices – one silver, one ornate with dragons – rarely used. I have a bell that was rung when I unboxed it and it has been silent ever since. I do, however, use my cauldron on a daily basis, but that is perhaps more to do with me having a liking for setting fire to things…

There are some wonderful tools on the market so do have a look around, but a lot of items can be handmade; wands in particular can be created from a stick found in the woods and don't forget to check charity/thrift stores as they often have a whole host of ornate chalices in the form of odd glasses or cups and brilliantly cheap cauldrons in the shape of casserole dishes costing a lot less than shop-purchased items.

Altar Cloth

This is useful in that it can add a bit of colour magic and also be tied in with the seasons. Altar cloths are sold with specific colours and patterns, but also have a look in charity/thrift stores for ladies' head scarves which work well or in fabric shops for offcuts and fat quarters of material. You don't need to have a cloth, but it does also serve a practical use in catching stray candle wax or spills.

Asperger

This is a weird name for a dish and a sprinkly thing. The dish holds water and the sprinkly thing...well sprinkles water over you or the space to cleanse and purify. It could be a feather or a brush or even a pine cone.

Athame

A ceremonial knife/dagger, double-edged, but not sharp (it is not usually used to physically cut anything). This is used in ritual to cast the circle, cut a doorway if necessary and to represent the male energy and the God, placed into the chalice to represent the ritual union.

Bell

A bell is sometimes used in ritual to welcome in the quarters or the deities or it can be used to help raise energy.

Besom

Besom is a gorgeous sounding word for a witch's broom, which is traditionally made from ash or birch and willow. What does a broom do? It cleans and that is exactly what a besom does, it is for cleansing the circle before ritual by sweeping. It is also used in hand fasting rituals for the happy couple to jump, symbolizing the end of their old life and the beginning of their new one...with a bit of fertility magic thrown in for good measure. If you have a lot of witches in ritual all with besoms they can also be placed end to end to create a circle...think about the scene from the movie Practical Magic...

Boline

Another knife, but unlike the athame this one is actually for cutting things – particularly herbs and plants for medicinal or magical use. Some of them are shaped as a crescent and often have a white handle. The Kitchen Witch in me suggests just using a vegetable knife...

Candles

What would a witch be without candles? Stuck really...candles are used a lot in magic not only for spell work, but also as representations of the deities, often a black candle for the God and a white candle for the Goddess, or for the element of fire. They are used to set light to petitions or just because let's face it a whole heap of candles looks pretty witchy.

Cauldron

One of my favourite tools and probably the one I use the most (back to the pyromaniac in me). The cauldron represents feminine energy and the womb, but it can also be used as a symbol for spirit or water and as a focus for the centre of your altar. It is also very sensible when you want to burn things whether it is candles, offerings or incense. A cauldron also holds liquids such as sacred water, potions or earth. If you have a traditional cast iron cauldron the three legs also symbolize the Goddess in her triple aspect and if it has two handles then that represents the God. As a substitute to a cast iron cauldron an old casserole dish or soup pot work very well.

Censer

I had never heard this word before I ventured into the realms of the Craft until I realized it is the brass thing on a chain that you see Roman Catholic Priests swinging about wafting smoke from. So that's what it is, a metal incense burner on a chain usually with sand in the bottom to absorb the heat. The censer is associated with the element of air.

Chalice

A vessel used to hold the ritual wine or mead and also representative of the feminine. It is used in Wiccan rituals in combination with the athame to symbolize the ritual union. You can get some very pretty and ornate chalices, but also take a look in charity/thrift stores for suitable alternatives.

Cords

Cords are used in initiations, knot magic and occasionally to mark the boundary of the circle.

Crystals

Perhaps a more modern tool used by witches but useful for all sorts of things, each crystal having its own magical and healing properties. They can also be used to represent the elements – each specific crystal aligning with one of the elements – but pebbles from the ocean or river can be also be used.

Crystal Ball

Often found on a witch's altar, it is used for divination obviously, but can also represent the Goddess. You can get the familiar larger crystal balls ala Gypsy Rose Lee, but you can also get smaller different coloured crystal balls. I have a green one and a hankering for a red one...

Deity Symbols

An altar usually has representations of the God and Goddess, the male and female energy. You can use candles, you can use beautiful statues, and you can also use crystals. I even have two pebbles from the beach on one of my altars that I painted symbols on to represent the God and the Goddess. You could even use a twig for the God and a pretty pebble for the Goddess, the options are limitless.

Drum

One of my favourite ways to raise energy or to meditate to, the drum beat is an amazing sound and feeling especially when you have a group of people all drumming in ritual. Inexpensive bodhran drums can be found as well as more expensive animal skin shamanic drums; African djembes, bongos or even a biscuit tin can also be used effectively. If you ever get the opportunity to birth your own drum I would highly recommend doing so. I spent a day birthing a stag skin drum and it was the most amazing, emotional and spiritual experience; and at the end of it I have a drum that is very personal to me, not only because I created it with my own hands, but also because we meditated beforehand to discover our drum spirit animal as well.

Horn

Very manly and Viking…ritual horns are usually made from stag antlers or bull horns. The latter are often used for the ritual drink filled with mead.

Incense

Incense comes in various forms; cones, sticks or loose. When at home I often use incense sticks, but in ritual we tend to use loose incense sprinkled on a charcoal disc. I love to create loose incense blends to tie in with the theme of the ritual or intent of magical work. You can use all sorts of ingredients just from your garden or kitchen cupboard, it doesn't have to be fancy schmancy expensive herbs from the other side of the globe. Incense is used in ritual to cleanse the sacred space, the circle or the people in the ritual; it is also a representation of the element of air.

Libation Bowl

Fancy word for offering bowl, kept on the altar to pop in water, wine, mead, herbs or whatever offering you feel is needed by deity (chocolate buttons if necessary, I know Ganesha is partial to sweeties). After the ritual the bowl is taken outside and poured onto the earth.

Lighter/Matches

Some traditions prefer to work with matches rather than lighters or vice versa. Matches are often used as they are more 'natural', but then lighters are sometimes preferred as they are sulphur free. I go with a lighter because it is more practical – anyone who has stood on top of a hill in a gale will know how difficult it is to light a charcoal disc with a lighter, let alone trying to light one with a match fighting against the wind.

Masks

Masks are sometimes worn in ritual by the High Priest/ess and in initiations or rites of passage. A green man mask is often worn for some sabbat rituals.

Mirrors

Dark mirrors are used for scrying, but can also act as portals. A dark mirror has a black surface, the expensive ones are made from ground obsidian, but you can easily make a very serviceable one by painting the back of the glass in a picture frame with a couple of coats of black paint. A mirror can also be used to direct sunlight or moonlight from outside onto any tools that need charging with their energy. The mirror is a symbol of the Goddess and also the element of water.

Mortar and Pestle

I always think this sounds like the name of a comedy duo...a mortar and pestle are incredibly useful if you are going to be making any incense blends or magical powders. One made from stone or wood is best, but failing that the end of a rolling pin and a small sturdy bowl work very well. If you are using non-edible or poisonous ingredients such as mistletoe berries please keep a separate magical pestle and mortar purely for that use. Don't grind up poisonous berries and then use it to make the spice rub for your chicken dinner...

Oils

An essential oil blend is sometimes used in ritual to anoint those in the circle, the High Priest/ess or those undertaking initiation. It can also be used to consecrate ritual tools.

Peyton (Altar Pentacle)

Never heard of the word? Nope neither had I. I believe it is a Wiccan/Gardnerian term for the altar pentacle. Sometimes in the form of a tile laid flat on the altar with a pentacle image on or a pentacle that is free-standing, it usually sits in the centre or towards the back of the altar. In ritual, it can be used to bless other tools or offerings. It represents the element of earth or spirit.

Rattle

A rattle can be used in ritual to clear away negative energy either from the ritual space or from people within the circle.

Salt

A bowl of salt is often kept on the altar to represent the element of earth or mixed with water for cleansing and purification. Sea salt is the variety of choice because it is natural and has not been processed, but table salt will do.

Scourge

Sounds medieval? Well it is really. The scourge is basically a ritual whip, although not often used now literally (as in taking skin from your back and drawing blood), it is used symbolically in some initiation rituals.

Sickle

Got a picture of Getafix the cartoon druidic Gaul in your mind? Well the crescent moon-shaped knife he had tucked into his belt that he used to harvest mistletoe was a sickle. It is worn by druids and represents the Moon.

Staff

Perhaps used more by druids than witches (although I have several), it can be used to cast the circle, direct energy or leant on during ritual if you get tired. We use a staff to pass around the circle in ritual as a talking stick. It can be as simple as a large stick found in the forest or a beautiful carved and inscribed staff or anything in between. I have one with a carved sea horse top, one with oak leaves carved all the way up and just a simple stang. A stang is a staff with a fork at the top (not a knife and fork...a V sign). The staff is a symbol of male energy and the God.

Sword

A sword can be used to cast the circle and used in initiation ceremonies – not for chopping off heads or anything sinister, but the seeker may be asked questions at sword point. The sword can be aligned with the element of fire or air.

Talking Stick

This does what it says on the tin. It is a stick that you pass around the circle and when you are holding it you can speak and everyone else has to listen.

Wand

Can be made from wood, crystal or metal and is used to cast the circle, invoking, banishing and directing energy. However, if you don't have a wand your pointy finger works as well. Different types of wood can be used for different magical workings and crystal wands are often used specifically for healing. The wand can be aligned with the element of fire or air.

Water

You can represent the element of water on your altar with…wait for it…a bowl of water! Although this is not advisable if you have small children or pets, cats in particular have a habit of being drawn to altars and will quite possibly drink your element of water.

Ritual Preparation and Techniques

Altar Layout

When I first started on this pathway I was studying Wicca, which has quite specific guidelines for laying out your altar tools. Over the years I have found my own way of doing things (probably because I don't like being told what to do much…) and I now put whatever I feel is right on my altar and in whatever order or position that my intuition tells me to. Go with the flow…it is your personal altar and must feel comfortable for you, unless you are part of a particular tradition that has specific guidelines of course. If you are leading an open ritual you may also prefer to stick to more traditional altar layouts or be prepared for people to question what you have done!

Below is an idea of the traditional placements to give you a starting point.

The suggestion is that your altar should face north or east, but you might not always be able to accommodate that, depending on what space you have in your house. If the only place you have is a shelf facing west then use it. The idea behind your altar facing north or east is that it should ideally be in the direction that you start casting your circle from. Witches often start in the north whereas Druids seem to favour starting in the east.

The Goddess goes on the left and the God on the right, so whatever representations you are using – whether they are statues, candles or whatever – should be placed accordingly. This goes with any feminine and masculine items too, so all items associated with the Goddess go on the left and the God on the right. Basically boobs and wombs on the left, willies on the right.

Then you have the elements. The four elements are earth, air, fire and water. Each one needs something to represent it and these should be placed at the corresponding compass points. Earth is at the north, air at the east, fire at the south and water at the west. (See the elements section for more details and suggestions). Some items are dual elements. For instance, incense could be air and fire so you might want to set it midway between the two directions of east and south.

Cleansing and Consecrating Your Tools

We cleanse and consecrate our magical tools to clear them of any negative energy that might be residing in them from previous owners, from the store they came from or just from the surrounding air. Do you want to use a magical tool that some snotty child has picked up in the store without cleansing it first? Nope didn't think so...ewwwww. We consecrate them to prepare them for magical work and to imbue them with our own energies and intent. You can work the cleansing and consecration of magical tools into a ritual to give them added oomph.

You don't want to use a magical tool that is carrying negative energies or unknown energies within it, as it will affect your working.

I'm not talking about popping on your rubber gloves and washing up here (although in the case of pebbles from the beach and the like it can be advisable); I am talking about spiritual cleansing.

There are several ways to cleanse a magical item and it will depend on what you have to hand and what the actual tool is made from.

Incense: You can pass an item through incense smoke to purify it. It is preferable to use a specific purifying scent such as sage, lavender or rosemary, but go with what feels right for you.

Breath: You can breathe on your tool, ground and centre yourself first and then really focus your breath on cleansing and purifying the item.

Weather: You can leave your tools outside, preferably on a windy day and let the air do the job for you. But keep an eye on them –

you don't want the dog to run off with your new athame and bury it somewhere.

Flame: You can pass items over the flame of a candle, but be very careful and make sure the item will not be damaged. You will need some visualisation skills for this one, to visualise the flame getting larger and enveloping the item to cleanse it.

Sunshine and Moonlight: You can also leave the item out in the Sun or under the Moon, allow the sunshine or moonlight to cleanse and purify it.

Water: You can wash the item in running water, under the tap or in a stream. You can also place the item in a bowl of water that has had a pinch of salt or a couple of drops of cleansing essential oil added to it. If you prefer you could use cooled herbal tea as the wash for your item. If the item is particularly delicate you can just sprinkle a few drops of salty water on it.

Burying: If the item is durable you can bury it either in the soil or in salt for a few hours (or days). The soil or the salt will absorb any negative energy. Oh and don't forget where you buried it...

Visualisation: The easiest way I think is to use your inner spirit. Take the object in your hands, call upon deity and visualise a cleansing and purifying white light coming through your hands and into the object, flushing out any negative energies from it and filling it with pure, clean energy.

Icky Stuff: If you feel it is your calling...you can consecrate items with your blood or bodily fluids. This works especially well with a drop of your blood on an athame or for divination tools such as runes. Menstrual blood or semen will help make a connection between you and your divination tool.

Once you have cleansed your magical tools you can bless or consecrate them. (Different words, same meaning).

You can consecrate an item by using the visualisation method mentioned above, sending the bright white light into the item and asking the Goddess and the God to bless it for magical work.

You can also say a blessing chant as well.

Tools and altar items, indeed your entire altar, should be cleansed and consecrated fairly regularly. I like to do it with the turning of the seasons, but if anything feels a bit hinky or you have used an item for specific spell work, give it a cleanse.

Intent and Purpose

You can perform a ritual just to give yourself some sacred time: cast a circle, call the quarters, invoke deity and sit and meditate, but rituals are usually set with a theme in mind. It might be to celebrate a sabbat or to work some specific magic or to work with or honour a particular deity.

Get your intent set first then plan out what you want to do or create. You can then tie everything into your intent and build the energy with correspondences. If your ritual is for a magical working to do with prosperity you can work extra bazinga into it by calling upon deities associated with prosperity and abundance, you can use colour magic in your altar cloth and candles, add in incense that ties in magical herbs associated with money and you are good to go. Keep the intent focused in your mind as you work through the ritual and don't forget to give thanks afterwards.

Devotions

I make a point of standing in front of my deity altar once a day, usually before I go to bed or first thing in the morning, and just spend a couple of minutes thanking deity and giving devotion to them and my pathway. It is just a way of giving thanks and reconnecting. If I am in need or know I am going to be facing a particularly difficult day I will also light some incense or a candle on the altar and say a few words, I don't want to use the word prayer because it has such a bad rep in the pagan world, but that is essentially what I am doing.

Clothing and Jewellery

I thought it important to mention here about clothing in particular. One of the statements I often hear is; 'I can't go to a ritual I don't have any ritual clothing.' And my answer is always; 'It doesn't matter what you wear, come in whatever you want to.'

As a High Priestess if I am leading a ritual then I do like to make a bit of an effort, I feel it is important in the position that I hold to not only look the part, but also to dress up to honour deity. In fact it is also a bit of a switch, dressing in specific ritual clothing helps me to tune into the occasion. I don't always wear a cloak because to be honest in the summer months it is often way too warm to wear one, but believe me in the winter it is a very nice addition to keep the cold out.

At the Kitchen Witch Coven, we have held a series of elemental rituals this year so I have made a point of wearing the corresponding colour outfit for the ritual, topped with a flower circlet. Nothing expensive, I purchased the flowers in a discount shop and made it myself, but just a couple of flowers from the garden tucked behind your ear works as well. Cloaks are expensive, they take a long time to make and a lot of material. However, a coloured throw can be used or a piece of curtain fabric, be inventive. But...if you don't own a cloak or robes please don't let it stop you from going to a ritual. However, there are some traditions that do require specific clothing to be worn, whether it is a particular colour cloak or for druidic groups it might be druid robes. It is worth asking beforehand.

Skyclad has to be mentioned here, it is a word used for performing a ritual completely stark naked, no clothes, nadda, not a stitch on. There is a camp of thought that says wearing clothes in ritual stops the flow of energy...my thoughts on that are 'tosh, absolute tosh...' And anyway I live in the UK...it is way too nippy here to be dancing about nekkid on top of a hill in this weather, I would catch my death of cold... However, if it appeals to you go for it, it may be incredibly liberating...just don't get arrested for indecent behaviour.

As for jewellery I have read on occasion warnings not to wear any bling in ritual that isn't real silver, gold or precious/semi precious stones because it stops the flow of energy...see my skyclad response above... Anyway moving on...often I will wear a necklace that represents my totem animal or a pendant with a semi-precious stone in because I require those particular energies. I also wear a necklace that represents my matron Goddess and patron God, but we are back to that personal choice thing again. If you feel you need to wear a specific piece of jewellery for ritual then do so, if you want to wear your bright pink plastic bubble necklace in ritual do so, follow your intuition.

Take a Bath...

If you want to do the whole shebang with a ritual you can start with yourself and taking a ritual bath is a way of purifying not only your physical body but also your mind. It is important not to step into circle with a whole heap load of mind chatter going on bringing your own stresses and worries with you because that will affect the energy of the ritual. Grounding and centring is a must, but using water in the form of a shower or bath works very effectively, bringing the refreshing, cleansing and purifying powers of water. You can also add in some herbs or chanting to your ritual wash if you want to.

Sacred Space

This term is thrown about a lot in paganism and although it does mean in part the actual physical space you use for ritual it is soooo much more. Sacred space is within you, around you as you walk, sleep and work – everything is sacred. Having an altar or creating a circle for ritual creates a focal point for that sacred space.

Physical Space

You need an area for the ritual, now this might be your living room, your garden, a clearing in your local forest or a sacred site. Wherever you choose to hold the ritual it needs some preparation. If it is indoors make sure you have room, move some furniture if you need to. If it is outside make sure the ground is clear (very embarrassing to be halfway through a ritual and step in dog poop). If you are limited on space just make sure there is enough room to stand or sit without knocking ornaments flying. While it is very special to be able to hold your ritual on a sacred site it is not necessary, the magic, energy and atmosphere created are down to you and those with you – a ritual in your back garden can be just as powerful as one on an ancient sacred place.

In some traditions the space that will be used for ritual is smudged with incense first or sprinkled with blessed water. The circle edge can also be swept with a besom to clear out any negative energies, this is symbolic as the bristles of the broom don't actually touch the ground. Sweeping should be done around the circle widdershins (anti-clockwise) to remove any energies that you don't want there.

Also remember that clutter and dust have a habit of harbouring negative energy, so if you are indoors give the place a bit of Snow White attention before you start your ritual.

You can also use visualisation to cleanse your sacred space just by seeing a pure white (or a colour of your choice) light clearing and cleansing the space.

If you are holding an open ritual please also bear in mind those who are less sure-footed and pick somewhere that is easily accessible and not a fourteen-mile hike from the car park...

Grounding and Centring

Performing a ritual or being part of one should be quite energising, so you need to ground and centre yourself afterwards, but I find it is also helpful to do so beforehand as well.

They are essentially two different things but often done together and become intertwined.

Grounding is such a simple practice, but can be so beneficial. Ever had one of those fruit loop days when you are all airy fairy? Grounding can sort that out and bring you back to connect with the earth. Connecting with the energy of the earth not only grounds us, but also brings us a special connection to the energy and strength that Mother Earth can provide. Being ungrounded can be extremely exhausting and very draining on your own energy resources, that chaotic and twirly feeling can kick in after a ritual if you don't ground and it can also give you a heck of a headache, either because you used too much of your own energy during ritual or spell work or because you have too much excess energy that you need to 'earth' back to the ground.

The most well known grounding exercise involves visualising yourself as a tree, any tree, it doesn't matter what sort. Take a deep breath in and out and relax. Visualise your feet becoming roots and sending them down into the ground. See the roots grow and push deeper into the soil. Allow any stresses and worries to empty out through your roots into the Earth. Then bring up some of the energy from the Earth's core back through your roots and up into your body allowing that energy to flow around your entire being. Allow any excess to flow back into the Earth and then when you are ready draw your roots back in. You should now be grounded.

Centring is all about finding your inner centre, that sweet spot in the middle of you which houses your inner being, the part that the magic flows from. It may not actually be the physical centre of your body, it will be different for everyone, it might be your solar plexus (belly button area), it might be your heart or it could be anywhere on your body that feels right for you.

This uses your visualisation skills again by seeing a white (or colour of your choice) light entering the top of your head originating from up in the sky somewhere. Then you need to see another beam of light coming from the Earth and entering your base chakra (bottom of your spine). Watch as the two beams of light meet somewhere in the middle and swirl together to create a ball of energy. Connect yourself with this central energy. This is your centre of being; this is where your control, calm, connection and general oomph comes from. When you are ready allow both beams to slowly withdraw and let the ball of energy dissipate as much as you want or need it to.

And that's it...simples. Both of these exercises are advisable before and after any ritual or magical workings, but they can also be done at any time of the day when you feel the need.

Eating something and drinking will also help you to ground, but you might want to place your palms face down on the ground and release any excess energy you have, or stomp your feet and clap your hands after a ritual as well.

Procession

I have been a part of many druidic rituals where we don't start in the circle; we form a line at a designated spot and walk in procession until we meet 'the gatekeeper' where we have to ask permission to enter the sacred space. Once the gatekeeper is assured that our intentions are honourable he allows everyone through, we process to the edge of the circle, turning and pausing to salute the Sun in the east then moving into the circle.

Cast the Circle

If you are just working on your own, meditating or doing a simple candle spell, I don't believe casting a circle is always necessary. If you regularly smudge and protect your house and have your own shielding in place, I would say don't bother, but the choice is yours. If you are going to be raising energy, especially if there is a group of you, then I would recommend casting a circle. If you are gathered together to celebrate a Sabbat especially then it's nice to 'put on the full works' too. Casting a circle puts up a protective barrier around you, it not only keeps out any unwanted negative energy but it also keeps the energy you are raising safely inside the circle until you release it. Casting a circle does, however, create a place 'between the worlds'. It is grounded in the physical, but also gives you a connection to the spiritual. It can also be a very safe, secure place especially if you need a bit of a spiritual hug, casting a circle and just 'being' inside it can be very uplifting.

Some witches will invoke the elements before casting the circle, others will cast the circle first; it's another one of those personal choice things.

Two words you will often hear when people refer to rituals: the first is deosil, which means clockwise or sunwise, and then widdershins, which means anti-clockwise. Basic rule of thumb is when you want to bring good energy or protection in you go deosil (clockwise) then when you want to dismiss something or banish negative energies you work widdershins (anti-clockwise). The circle is cast deosil and the quarters are called deosil, always move around the circle in a deosil motion. The circle and quarters are then usually released widdershins.

To cast a circle you can use an athame, a sword, a wand, a staff or just your finger, it is a personal choice. Walk deosil (clockwise) around the circle with your arm outstretched, visualise a bright white light coming from your arm and creating a circle. You can go further with this and make the circle come up and over you in a dome shape and even under you to form a complete bubble. You can also add colours to the visualisation too. You can chant as you cast the circle.

When we hold open rituals at the Kitchen Witch Coven, we scatter herbs as we walk the circle, often rose petals but also herbs that correspond to the intent of the ritual. Never scatter any material on the ground that is not biodegradable please!

You walk completely around the circle until you come back to where you started, if it is a small circle and you want to use a longer chant you can walk the circle three, six or nine times.

If there are a group of you, the circle can be cast with all of you linking hands and walking the circle together; this works well with a chant to accompany the walking.

The circle is a sacred symbol and one that is used worldwide. It has no beginning and it has no end, it is never ending, it is infinite. It is also the shape of the Earth, the Sun, the Moon in fact all of the planets. It is a symbol of life itself. When everyone stands in circle they all stand equally, there is no 'head of the table'. A circle is also a boundary; it marks the edge of your sacred ritual space.

There are several trains of thought about the circle itself. Some will cast the circle and it will be a rigid barrier. If you forget something and need to step outside of the circle a 'doorway' must be cut in the circle usually with an athame to allow you out and then closed once you are back inside. Others (like our coven) cast the circle wide and view it as a flexible 'bubble' that covers us if we need to step away from the circle to get something (usually the cake...). There is also the view that each person has their own protective circle that moves with them. Go with your intuition and what feels right for you.

The circle is usually held in place with visualisation as a circle of energy, but you can mark it in the physical realm as well. Besoms end-to-end look quite dramatic, but cords also work well or circles of flower petals or leaves – although that only works when it isn't windy! Crystals or pebbles can also be placed around the circle or a good ol'-fashioned ring of salt.

And then there are groups that choose not to cast a circle at all believing that the act of coming together in ritual brings sacred space with it or by using the same area all the time nature is its own sacred space.

Perfect Love and Perfect Trust

This is a bit of a sketchy area, the phrase was mentioned in a book by Gerald Gardner, who popularised Wicca, and has appeared in several poems and redes since, but I suspect the notion was around before then.

Some traditions will ask you; 'How do you enter this circle?' Before they will let you into the ritual space you are required to answer; 'In perfect love and perfect trust.' The idea being that once you enter the ritual circle that you are sharing that space with respect to everyone else, some of whom may be nervous or vulnerable, you are saying that by agreeing to the question asked you bring respect and trust with you and that you will show the same to your fellow members of the circle. It is a way of making people feel safe and secure within ritual.

Please bear in mind that not all pagans follow the guideline…

As Above, So Below

You may have heard this phrase in pagan groups: 'As above, so below; as within, so without.' The adage is traditionally attributed to the Emerald Tablet of Hermes Trismegistus:

That which is below corresponds to that which is above, and that which is above corresponds to that which is below, to accomplish the miracle of the One Thing.

All systems of magic are said to work using this formula. What is above is the same as that which is below. The universe is the same as the divine, the divine is the same as man, man is the same as the cell etc. What is above us is below us, what is inside us is outside as well. Basically we are all connected, everything to everything else. We use this connection with our will and energy to create magic and change. Deep huh?

Blessed Be

'Blessed be' is another term you will hear used in ritual (and outside by pagans). It is often used instead of a thank-you when you are offered food or drink in ritual and as a reply to a greeting. Loosely translated it means that you wish the person good and positive blessings.

So Mote It Be

The phrase, 'So mote it be,' is used to finalise something whether it is a spell or a working either on your own or in ritual. It does always make me think of Star Trek and Jean Luc Picard saying; 'Make it so,' which is essentially what it means – get it done! It may have its origins in old Saxon the word 'mote' meaning 'must', but it also has a history within Freemasonry where it means 'amen' or 'as God wills it to be'.

Calling for Peace

In a lot of druid rituals the call for peace is made, which is such a lovely idea. Someone will walk to each cardinal point, starting with the east, and state out loud, 'Let there be peace in the east,' to which the others within the circle reply, 'There is peace in the east.' They then move on to the next direction and give the call again, 'Let there be peace in the South.' It goes around until peace has been called in all four directions. It is a call for peace within the circle, the group and each person within. To define and use a space for ritual there needs to be peace within it.

Calling in the Quarters

Calling in the elements, calling the quarters, calling the Guardians of the Watchtowers, calling the elementals – so many names! But essentially we are calling upon the four elements from the four directions to join us in ritual and to lend their power, energy and protection. These might be in the form of literally just inviting the elements in or it could be members of the Faerie world such as elementals or something like dragons, but even then you would usually call in dragons that correspond to the four elements.

The elements are earth, air, fire and water. They are associated with the four compass directions: north, east, south and west.

The Guardians, sometimes called Guardians of the Watchtowers are the Guardians of the elements. They too share the characteristics of the elements they are associated with. They are not Gods, but they are otherworldly.

You can also call upon dragon magic and invite dragon energy to each quarter or you could call upon four Archangels. In a more shamanic or Native American style of ritual you might choose to call in the energy of animals to represent each quarter.

Anyone can call upon the elements or call the quarters. If you are a solitary, obviously you will do all the ritual procedures yourself, but if you are part of a group usually members of the circle (rather than the High Priest/ess or Arch Druid) will call the quarters, one for each element.

The elements are called in turn, you will find that most witches start in the north with earth which represents the Goddess as Mother Earth, but druids tend to start with air in the east because the Sun rises in the east. The person will turn and face the direction they are calling to and recite a chant requesting the presence of that element/elemental/quarter to join them in the ritual to add their power and energy to the rite. In Wiccan rituals the person will sometimes draw an invoking pentagram in the air at the same time.

Each element is then called in turn until all four have been called upon.

Some rituals will have a candle at each direction point, which will be lit when the element has been called, this works well if you are at home, but isn't overly practical on a windy hilltop unless you have very good hurricane lanterns.

What we sometimes do in our group rituals is pass the talking stick around the circle asking each member to say a word that they relate or associate with each particular element, so for instance with the element of fire people might say: passion, volcano, energy, bonfire etc.

The elements exist in everything and you can quantify them by saying air is the wind, fire is a volcano, but the elements are pure – they exist in the elemental realms. We can't go there, but they are places of energy vibration that intersect with our reality. They are the forces of the entire universe and create the basis of magic. The elements aren't just represented by physical effects, they also encompass feelings and emotions. Something like passion and creativity would correspond to the element of fire and emotions are connected with the element of water.

Elementals are categorised within the group of Faerie beings that are associated with the four elements. Gnomes are earth, slyphs are air, salamanders are fire and undines are water. The elementals are powerful beings and each carries with it the characteristics of the element it is associated with. I think perhaps that the true base elementals are far more raw and undefined than some would believe, but again it is only personal experience that can help you decide.

As with most things, the elementals have a hierarchy. Not everyone subscribes to this belief, but I will share it with you so that you have the details. Each element has a Guardian, a king, a ruler if you will. Some traditions will have given names for the Guardians of each element or each Watchtower, but essentially each Guardian stands guard at the gateway to the element it represents, once you call in that quarter the Guardian will open the door and allow the energy for that element to join you in ritual. The Guardian not only controls the gateway and whether it opens or closes, but also regulates how much energy is required for your ritual.

You could, of course, call in deities for each of the quarters, all

Gods and Goddesses are associated with one (or sometimes two) of the elements.

I don't think it matters what exact wording you use to call in the quarters; it doesn't have to rhyme or be overly dramatic or poetic, but always be respectful. Most people will end each quarter call with the words 'hail and welcome' and in a group ritual this is repeated by those in circle.

Don't forget your visualisation skills for this part of the ritual, as you (or whoever it might be in circle) call in each element really use your third eye skills and see and feel that element entering the circle in all its glory. There are lots of ways to visualise this: see the gateway opening, see the Goddess/ guardian/animal spirit at each direction, see the element itself or feel the element.

Each element also has a magical tool associated with it, so you could place that item at each direction. A pentacle would represent earth, an athame for air, a wand for fire and a chalice for water. You could also use simple representations such as soil or salt for earth, incense for air, a candle for fire and water for water.

You will also find in group ritual that people will tend to turn and face the direction that is being called in, often with their arms down but palms facing front and hands open. Once a quarter has been called they will turn and face the next direction. You could also hold your arms in the air with hands turned upwards.

Arm movements can be used very effectively when calling in the quarters such as using spirals; using your receptive hand to start the spiral in the centre and move outwards in a clockwise motion. Do this three times as you call in the quarter. Use your other hand and work anti-clockwise to dismiss the quarter at the end of the ritual.

You could also draw elemental symbols in the air at each quarter, or if you are standing on soil or sand you could even draw them on the floor, but perhaps not in marker pen on the carpet... Earth is an inverted triangle with a line horizontally through it, air is an upright triangle with a line across, water is an inverted triangle and fire is an upright triangle.

At the end of the day, do what works for you and sometimes less is more and the simpler you keep it the better it can work. If you are working with a solitary ritual you can just turn to each direction, close your eyes and visualise the element in your mind's eye; no need for words even or any arm waving at all.

At one of our group rituals we decided to do something a bit different (as is our want) and we got the four quarter callers to take one step into the circle away from the edge, as each one called their element in they held one end of a piece of coloured ribbon. I then took the other end and walked it into the centre of the circle where I tied it to the cauldron. I did the same for each caller with a different colour ribbon for each element. When all four elements had been called in, I walked to the centre and tied all four ends of ribbon together, binding the four elements to make the fifth element of spirit.

Be careful when calling in the Fae as they can be a bit naughty and make sure you ask them to leave when you have finished otherwise they can hang around and cause chaos...bless their cotton socks...

I have listed the four elements against the compass directions that I was taught and that I am comfortable with, but it doesn't make them set in stone; if you prefer to work with them in a different position then go with what feels right for you. I think you also have to work with the location you are in; if you are on the beach and the ocean is on your right, i.e. in the position of east, it would seem far more sensible to work with that as your direction for water.

You can see some examples of quarter calls in the ritual suggestions part of this book.

Playing with Pentagrams

Often used in Wiccan and ceremonial rituals, the pentagram –

the five pointed star (pentacle is the five pointed star with a circle around the edge) – is drawn in the air at each direction; invoking to bring in the element and banishing to release it.

The invoking pentagram is drawn using five strokes (or lines) and depending on what element you are invoking will decide where you start drawing. So to invoke earth you would start at the top point of the pentagram and draw downwards to the left first, to invoke fire you would start at the top of the pentagram and draw downwards to the right first. Invoking air starts at the right hand point and goes across to the left and invoking water starts at the left hand point and goes across to the right. For all elements you then continue drawing the pentagram in a continuous stroke until you reach your start point, or you can add an extra stroke and repeat the first line to make a total of six strokes. It sounds complicated, but once you get the hang of it really it is very simple, I promise. It is then drawn in reverse at the end of the ritual to dismiss the quarters. Some traditions draw a clockwise circle around the pentagram to invoke and draw it anti-clockwise to banish.

You can keep it simpler by using the same start point for all elements, so to invoke you would start at the top, draw down to the left point, then over to the right side. Draw straight across to the left side, draw down to the right point then sweep up to the top. To devoke you would start at the top and draw down to the right point, then over to the left side. Draw straight across to the right side then down to the left point then sweep up to the top.

At first you might look like you are trying to swat a swarm of invisible flies, but with practise you will get the hang of it.

Let's Look at the Elements...

For pagans the elements make up the universe, pretty much everything can be broken down and placed in one of the element groups. Personality types, seasons, altar tools, directions, astrological signs, animals, herbs, plants, tarot cards and crystals all have a corresponding element.

Earth

What do you think of when you visualise earth? The brown stuff that you plant things into in your garden? Grass, fields, mountains, valleys or rocks? Soil contains and stores all the minerals and moisture that plants need to survive. Earth is everything we are and everything we have comes from this element. We are born from it and we return to it when we die.

Earth is associated with abundance and prosperity, which makes sense as the earth is what provides us with food and nourishment. But it is also the rocks and stone, it is quite basically the total foundation of our planet. It is grounding and stabilising.

Earth is associated with north, with the season of winter and the advancement of old age. Winter, to me at least, is a time of reflecting. The trees and plants and even the animals have all withdrawn into Mother Earth to recuperate, to replenish, ready to venture forth in the spring, renewed and refreshed. Don't forget to look after this element, the planet, the environment around you. It can even be something small like picking up a piece of litter.

Earth has the colours of the season of winter; those of the dark nights, brown soil, dark grassy landscapes and the white of frost and snow.

The tool associated with earth is stone in the form of a pentacle or a bowl of soil or salt and it equates to the power of 'to know'.

To represent this element you could use a small dish of soil, an earthenware dish, a stone, a pebble, a crystal or even a piece of wood.

Direction: North
Nature: Fertile, nurturing, stabilising, grounding
Elemental: Gnome
Archangel: Uriel
Deity: Gaia, Ceres, Persephone, Demeter, Pan, Danu, Dagda, Osiris, Modron, Cernnunos
Gender: Feminine
Colours: Green, brown, black, grey, white
Places: Caves, forests, groves, valleys, fields, farms, gardens, parks, kitchens, basements, mines, holes
Magic: Money, prosperity, fertility, stability, grounding, employment, material matters, binding, grounding, manifesting, and healing
Herbs/Plants: Patchouli, vertivert, moss, nuts, roots, barley, cotton, cypress, fern, honeysuckle, horehound, knotweed, mugwort, oats, potato, primrose, rhubarb, rye, sorrel, tulip, turnip, wheat
Stones: Emerald, peridot, agate, apache tear, aventurine, orange calcite, carnelian, diamond, fluorite, jade, jasper, jet, malachite, petrified wood, ruby, sugilite, tiger eye, black or green tourmaline, unakite
Metals: Iron, lead
Music: Drum, percussion
Animals: Dog, horse, earthworm, gopher, ant, cow, burrowing animals, wolf, bear
Season: Winter
Time: Night
Tool: Pentacle
Signs: Taurus, Virgo, Capricorn

Sense: Touch
Symbols: Salt, clay, soil, rocks, wheat, acorns
Tarot: Pentacles (discs/coins)

Air

Air is perhaps the most difficult element to visualise because you can't really see it. But think of a bright blue sky with wispy white clouds or the wind gently moving the branches of a tree.

Air is all about intellect, truth and knowledge. Air means truth, truth in who you really are and the freedom that comes with that realisation.

Think about the qualities of the wind too, when it whips up the leaves and sends them dancing around. When a wisp of breeze catches your hair. There is nothing quite like the feeling of standing on top of a windy hill with your arms outstretched just letting the wind wrap around you. Don't forget that air also has a destructive side, think of hurricanes and tornadoes.

Air represents east, the season of spring and youth. It is the place of hope and new beginnings. We get up, we start each new day fresh with new opportunities to learn and grow. We go out into the world to go about our business.

Spring has the same feeling – fresh, new energy. We have hibernated over winter, dreaming and planning. Now it is time to put those plans into action.

Youth is an exciting and even slightly scary time. We set out on our own, starting to explore the big world for ourselves. New experiences, new people, new ventures. This is the time when we start to discover who we are.

Air is associated with thoughts. We need air to breathe, and therefore to live. The air we breathe in allows us to think clearly, to clear our minds.

Air has the colours of spring: the yellow of the rising Sun, the light blue of the sky and white of the clouds. Even pale green and pink of new foliage and blossom of Bride (sometimes spelled

Brighid or Brigit), the Goddess of Spring.

The tool most often associated with air is the athame or incense and it equates to the power of 'to dare'. The blade (as in the athame) represents truth. The blade of an athame is traditionally double edged to symbolize that the power of a witch can cut both ways.

To represent the element of air you might like to use feathers, incense or spring flowers.

Direction: East (sometimes south)
Nature: Flying, moving, intelligence
Elemental: Sylph
Archangel: Raphael
Deity: Arianrhod, Thoth, Anubis, Inanna, Zeus, Hera, Thor, Odin, Llud, Isis
Gender: Male
Colours: Yellow, pale blue, pink, light green
Places: Mountain tops, plains, cloudy skies, high towers, airports, schools, libraries, offices, travel agents
Magic: Travel, instruction, study, freedom, knowledge, recovering lost items, creativity, visions, psychic power, divination, visualisation, communication, truth
Herbs/Plants: Flowers, agaric, agrimony, anise, benzoin, bergamot, bittersweet, borage, bracken, brazil nut, broom, caraway, chicory, dock, endive, fenugreek, hazel, hops, lemongrass, mace, maple, marjoram, meadowsweet, mint, mistletoe, palm, parsley, pecan, pine, rice, sage, slippery elm
Stones: Pumice, mica, amethyst, azurite, beryl, blue lace agate, carnelian, chrysoprase, citrine, diamond, fluorite, moldivite, opal, pearl, snow quartz, sapphire, sodalite, blue topaz, blue tourmaline, turquoise
Metals: Tin, copper
Music: Flute, wind instruments
Animals: Spider, birds, winged insects

Season: Spring or summer
Time: Dawn
Tool: Athame or wand
Signs: Gemini, Libra, Aquarius
Sense: Hearing, smell
Symbols: Feathers, incense, flowers
Tarot: Swords

Fire

Well, the visualisation for this one couldn't be simpler really, flames. But I also see bonfires and a warm cosy log fire.

Fire brings warmth, comfort and protection. It is the light in the dark that drives away outside threats. Fire brings people together, as a community. Although most houses now don't have open fires in each room, a lot still have fireplaces. The hearth is the centre of a home.

Fire is passion; it is the burning flame inside that gives us passion, energy and strength. It is the fire within us that helps us to meet the challenges that life brings to us. Fire also sparks our imagination, lights our passions and fills us with enthusiasm and encouragement. Fire is also the element that gives us our ooh la la and va va voom.

Fire can also be destructive, but in that destruction comes renewal and rebirth – think of the phoenix rising from the ashes. The warning that comes with fire is that it does need to be kept in check. A fire that causes rage can get out of hand.

Cast your mind to the blacksmith's forge. The blacksmith takes raw material, heats it in the fire and creates something new from it. A transformation; this we can do with our own selves.

The fire within you is your own personal power. It is the force that gives you confidence, it takes away the fear and challenges you to push yourself that bit further.

Fire represents the south, the season of summer and adulthood. The Sun is at its highest point, it is when we put all our energy into projects and help them to grow and mature. The projects that were started in the spring are now flourishing. It is a time for energy, activity and passion. A time to laugh, dance, sing and have fun.

Adults have experience, experience of life and who they are. By adulthood you should have found your place in the world. You have responsibilities, control of your life and your expectations. Just remember to enjoy yourself too, find your inner passion and run with it!

Fire is the colour of summer: the reds of a beautiful sunset, the yellow of the Sun and even the green and bright colours of summer flowers and plants. I think of Belenos the Celtic Sun God.

Fire equates to the power of will; this is your ability to direct the energy needed and your focus out into the big ol' universe to create the magic that you want. The main tool that is represented by fire is a wand, which is why it works well to cast a circle and work magic as it directs and focuses your energy and therefore your 'will'.

To represent fire the most obvious item is a candle, especially a red one. You could also use a red stone/crystal.

Direction: South (sometimes east)
Nature: Purifying, destructive, cleansing, energetic, sexual, forceful, will, passion, power, intense, movement, drive, soul
Elemental: Salamander
Archangel: Michael
Deity: Solar Gods such as Ra, Apollo, Helios, Brighid, Hestia, Oak King, Freya, Balder – warrior and war Gods are associated with fire too
Gender: Male
Colour: Red
Places: Desert, hot springs, volcano, oven, fireplace, bedroom, locker room, sauna, sports field

Magic: Protection, courage, sex, energy, strength, authority, banishing, negativity, passion, will, movement

Herbs/Plants: Stinging nettle, thistle, chilli, cactus, coffee, seeds, alder, allspice, anemone, angelica, ash, basil, bay, betony, chrysanthemum, cinnamon, clove, coriander, cumin, curry, dill, dragon's blood, fennel, carnation, carrot, cashew, cedar, fig, frankincense, garlic, ginger, hawthorn, juniper, lime, lovage, mandrake, marigold, mustard, nutmeg, oak, orange, holly, rosemary, pepper, pomegranate, tobacco, walnut, witch hazel, woodruff

Stones: Jasper, lava, quartz, amber, beryl, bloodstone, gold calcite, carnelian, citrine, coal, diamond, geodes, red jasper, obsidian, peridot, smoky quartz, rhodochrosite, sunstone, yellow topaz

Metals: Gold, brass

Music: Guitar, stringed instruments

Animals: Snake, cricket, lizard, bee, scorpion, shark, fox, lion, ram, horse

Season: Summer (sometimes spring)

Time: Noon

Tool: Wand, athame, candle

Signs: Aries, Leo, Sagittarius

Sense: Sight

Symbols: Flames, lava, candles

Tarot: Wands

Water

With water my first thought is always of the ocean, of waves crashing on the shore.

What would we do without water? It sustains all life. Without water we and all the plants and animals would not survive. Water is very powerful – the ocean, a flood, a tidal wave. Water is all about emotions. Emotions flow, chop and change and rise to the surface as water does in a river, lake or ocean, so water is also an element that covers the aspects of love. A shower of rain can be refreshing like the release of emotion or destructive like the waves on a rough sea.

Water is also cleansing and healing. We clean ourselves, wash our food, and clean our houses and possessions with water. Your daily household chores, such as washing up, can be cleansing rituals in themselves.

Water is excellent for scrying. Divination with water uses our intuition, imagination and emotions. Take a bowl that has a dark inside, fill it with water and drop a silver coin in the bottom. Calm and centre yourself, look into the water and see what images come to you.

Water represents the west. It is the season of autumn and old age. This is the time of harvest, a time to gather in. What we have spent the year nurturing and tending to is now ready to reap. It is time to let go.

As people get older and become more aware of their mortality, they seek to balance their lives. They surrender some of the hard work they have been doing and concentrate on what is most important to them. Often these are things that bring emotional fulfilment, like spending time with loved ones, or pursuing a creative dream.

Water gives us the flow of our emotions and nurtures our lives. In return, we can offer it our love. Everything we do with love, and every act of love we perform, honours water. Love, like water, has the power of healing.

The colours of water are the colours of the sea: the blue of the Mediterranean, and the grey of the North Sea. The black of a deep lake and the green of the sea before a storm. But also all the glorious colours of the autumn leaves that remind me of the God Mabon

Water equates to the power of keeping silent. The chalice is the tool that is associated mostly with water along with the cauldron. Both are also symbols of the womb and the Goddess; they are very feminine.

On my altar, a bowl of water with sea shells represents water. For my magical work I use a simple earthenware cup. It holds the water I collected at Brigit's well or healing tinctures and teas that I want to use. It helps me to hold the power of magic, but its waters also bless and cleanse the circle. I use it in meditation when I want to feel my emotions clearly.

The fruit of a plant is filled with water that makes it juicy. Fruit collects the water so that the seed has the moisture it needs to germinate. In autumn it ripens and is ready for harvest, at the peak of its flavour.

Direction: West
Nature: Flowing, purifying, healing, soothing, loving
Elemental: Undine
Archangel: Gabriel
Deity: Water Gods such as Danu, Ereshkigal, Poseidon, Aphrodite, Maannan and Nuada
Gender: Female
Colour: Blue
Places: Lake, spring, stream, river, beach, ocean, well, swimming pool, bath, shower, fountain
Magic: Purification, love, psychic awareness, dreams, sleep, peace, marriage, friends, emotions, subconscious, healing
Herbs/Plants: Aloe, apple, aster, lemon balm, birch, blackberry, burdock, cabbage, camellia, caper, cardamom, catnip, chamomile, chickweed, coconut, coltsfoot, columbine, cowslip, cucumber, daffodil, daisy, elder, elm, eucalyptus, feverfew, gardenia, heather, hemlock, iris, larkspur, lemon, lettuce, lilac, mallow, morning glory, myrrh, pansy, peach, plum, rose, sandalwood, sea weed, tansy, thyme, tomato, valerian, water lily, willow, yarrow, yew
Stones: Amethyst, aquamarine, blue tourmaline, beryl, calcite, chalcedony, diamond, emerald, jade, jet, kunzite, lapis lazuli,

magnetite, moonstone, obsidian, onyx, opal, peridot, rose quartz, rock crystal, blue topaz, pink tourmaline, zircon
Metals: Mercury, silver, copper
Music: Cymbal, bell, chimes
Animals: Cat, frog, turtle, dolphin, whale, otter, seal, fish, shellfish
Season: Autumn
Time: Dusk
Tool: Chalice, cauldron
Signs: Cancer, Scorpio, Pisces
Sense: Taste
Symbols: Shells, water
Tarot: Cups

Spirit

There is the fifth element, that of spirit. To me it encompasses all the others, but here are some basic correspondences:

Direction: All four – north, east, south, west and also within, without, up and down
Nature: Unknowable
Colours: Purple, black
Places: Space, vacuum, voids
Metal: Meteoritic
Time: Eternal

Just a note here about some of the confusion in elements in particular with air and fire. Some say that air is represented by an athame others say it is a wand. That then affects fire, which can be a wand or an athame. If you believe a wand is used for focusing your will and that it is a source of power and protection then use it for fire. If, however, you believe the wand is a tool to channel your intuition and intellect then it should be a tool of air. The athame or the blade can symbolise the power of thought, our razor-sharp mind, cutting words or the sharpness of a tongue – if that's how you see it then it would be a tool of air. If you see the blade as a tool of action, anger and aggression, one that directs your will, then you would use it as a tool of fire. Go with what works for you.

The Three Worlds

And then there are those who don't call in the four quarters, but work with the three worlds instead (often those who follow the Norse path). The three worlds or three realms are made up from the land, the sea and the sky with the sacred fire being the centre.

The three worlds make perfect sense to me; the land sustains us and keeps us grounded, the sea provides sustenance and is a connection to the Otherworld and is a very powerful element, then the sky watches over us and holds the Moon, the Sun and the stars and of course the Gods. In the centre of all these is the sacred fire that binds them all together.

The three worlds can be invited into ritual by singing, chanting, drumming or just asking.

Invite Deity

Invoking/Evoking

Two very confusing terms: invoking and evoking – so what is the difference? To be honest in our coven we often just refer to it as 'calling in'.

Invocation and evocation are often used interchangeably and both words are apparently derived from the Latin word *'vocare'*, which means 'to call forth'. Both words mean to summon something nonhuman. But is there a difference? Evocation is used to call an entity forth, but in such a way that the practitioner is not linked to them, you invite deity/spirit to join you, but you still have control. With invocation the practitioner becomes a vessel, inviting the entity to come forth into them, giving control over to the deity/spirit; basically you invite them into your body/head. So the bottom line is invocation is calling into and evocation is calling forth – confused yet?

Why Do We Invite Deity?

Usually deity is invited to join a ritual; which ones to invite is, again, personal choice. Some groups may only work with specific deities whatever ritual they are performing, some will work with deities specific to the sabbat, some will call upon an all-encompassing deity and just invite 'The Lord and Lady' to join the rite. In coven rituals the Goddess and the God are often invited in by the High Priest or the High Priestess, but of course again if you are a solitary you will be doing all the calling. If you don't work with deity you could just call upon Mother Earth and Father Sky, or you don't have to include deity in your ritual at all.

Why invite deity? Well there are many reasons; we want to honour them, we would like them to witness the ritual, we would like them to enjoy the ritual, we ask for their wisdom, guidance and protection, we would like them to receive our offerings, we would like them to add their energy to our workings and to give us their blessings. The Gods can help teach us valuable lessons; they can influence our magical workings, increase our knowledge and inner strength and be there for us when we need support. But they also force us to take responsibility for our own actions and have a habit of kicking butt when necessary...

Bear in mind that each and every person may have a different perspective on deity and the divine, no one is wrong, no one is right, it just is. There are many, many aspects to deity and the divine from the Gods in all their various pantheons (some of which are decidedly similar across the cultures) from nature spirits, to angels to demons. Most pagans (and I say most, this isn't the case for everyone) will have a polytheistic belief, which means instead of one God we have a whole heap load of them. My thoughts are these...deity is a huge multifaceted diamond, as one it is the divine (for me the Goddess, but with both feminine and masculine energies), but each facet is a different personality of deity which translate into all the different pantheons and deities therein. Of course...just because I believe it does not make it the ultimate answer.

I work with the Gods to support me in my spiritual journey. Over the years I have worked with many different pantheons and even more individual deities, each one has come to me for a particular reason to share their own unique energies, character- istics and wisdom. I haven't always liked what they had to say or show me and sometimes I have fought against it, but ultimately they have been there to do what was best for me.

Some traditions will only invite a Goddess into the ritual, preferring to work only with the feminine energy and this works well, especially in women-only covens, Moon circles and red tent rituals. In all of our coven rituals we bring in both the Goddess and the God so that we have a balance. As we have both male and female members in the ritual it is how we prefer to work.

Who Do You Call?

As with most pagan questions there are many answers (fighting my inner 1980s' child who wants to answer with 'Ghostbusters'). If you work with a specific pantheon then you might want to stick with deities within that group. If you are working a ritual for a specific sabbat you may choose to work with deities that correspond with the celebration of, for instance, harvest Gods and Goddesses at Lughnasadh and dark Gods and Goddesses at Samhain. If you are working a ritual with an intent such as prosperity you might want to invite deities that are associated with money and abundance.

One of the subjects that often comes up is, 'Can I mix pantheons?' I can only answer this from personal experience... I have stuck with deities from the same pantheon and all has been fine and dandy, but I have also mixed and matched. In fact my matron Goddess is Celtic and my patron God is Hindu, not the most obvious of pairings, but they tolerate each other. The rituals held by my coven tend to be written by a team of people, each one will make a suggestion for a deity they would like to call in, so for each ritual we have four deities; two Goddesses and two Gods and we have had a totally mixed bag of pantheons. I can report that so far other than a bit of rain we haven't suffered any bolts of lightning or plagues of locusts. So my recommendation would be to go with your intuition and what works for you. What I would suggest is make sure you know at least a little bit of background about the deities you intend to work with before you invite them in. You may not want to invite a powerful warrior God in for a love ritual...

How Do You Call Them?

So you are ready to send out the party invites to the Lord and Lady, what do you do now? You know that I am going to say it's up to you and personal choice, right? However, there are traditional ways of doing so. Whichever way you end up doing it always be respectful. A bellow of; 'Oi you lot get over here,' will either be ignored or you will pay for it.

Usually the male and female are invited separately. Invite them using their name, their title and say something about their reputation and the specific characteristics they bring with them. Basically flatter them. Each invite is usually finished with; 'Hail and welcome!'

You will see different examples of deity evocations in the ritual suggestions section of this book.

Ancestors

Some traditions will also invite their ancestors to join the ritual, or the spirits of the land. It could be their own specific ancestors (i.e. grandparents), but it could also be the ancestors of their people so it might be Celtic spirits for instance. It could also be the ancestors of the land that you are standing on, especially if you are outside in a forest or at a sacred place.

Water, Incense, Oil, Wine and Kisses

Water and Incense

Some traditions will have a member of the group go around the circle smudging everyone with cleansing and purifying incense. They may also have someone go around the circle to bless everyone with water (the posh name is asperging).

Water is easy to use and create because you can just use tap water with a sprinkling of salt in. If you want to be more fancy you can use spring water mixed with sea salt or you can create your own sacred Moon water by popping a dish of spring water outside in the light of the Full Moon, add a bit more magic to your water by dropping a silver coin in the bowl. Sun water can be created in much the same way by leaving a dish of spring water outside in the sunlight and a gold coin can be added. Blessed water can also be collected from sacred springs or from the ocean; just give your thanks or perhaps leave an offering when you collect it, then ask for blessings from the divine for your water. If you are feeling really industrious you can also collect dew from the plants in your garden first thing in the morning.

One thing to remember about using salt water is that it is used to banish energies and spirits, so if you are hoping to call upon the spirits of your ancestors and you have sprinkled the circle with salt water they may not be too keen to enter…

Once you have your bowl of blessed water you can just dip your fingers in and flick it at people…lots of fun, but can get out of hand…or you can use a handful of leaves/small piece of tree branch to dip into the water and flick or a pine cone also works well.

Smudging is another method for cleansing not only people or space in ritual, but also for tools, crystals, homes or anything that needs a bit of a spiritual clear out. You can use incense sticks or cones or create a loose blend on charcoal. You could also use smudge sticks, which are often made from bundles of sage, but I like to add in lavender and rosemary too. I suggest using a purifying scent such as sage, frankincense, juniper, star anise, lavender, pine, citrus or rosemary. These are just some suggestions, but be guided by your own intuition. We often create a specific incense blend that corresponds to the intent of the ritual or uses ingredients that are associated with the deities we will be working with.

The smoke from the incense can be wafted either using your hand or feathers up, down and around each body when in ritual.

Kernips or Lustral Water

This is a lovely way of cleansing not only the people in ritual, but also the sacred space, shared with us by Samantha Leaver our coven's Hellenic witch.

You will need a sprig of rosemary, salt water in a bowl and a white towel.

It happens before the ritual starts, before the quarters (if you're calling them, certainly before the deities and definitely before magic). The Greeks believed in something called 'miasma', which is a general term for impurities, Before any special occasions, especially rituals, they made a point of getting ritually purified of miasma by making kernips or lustral water. This is the Hellenic version of smudging the circle. The point with rosemary is that it's cleansing, but really any burning herb will do. An herb that has the specific intent of the ritual would also be good.

What to do: mix the salt in the water, light the rosemary with a match. Extinguish the rosemary in the water. If the rosemary won't light, extinguish the match in the water and dip the rosemary in. Say: 'May this water be made pure under the eyes of the (immortal) Gods.' (It is up to you if you want to say immortal).

Take it round clockwise finishing with the Priestesses/Priests running the festivities. Tell them to dip their forefinger and middle fingers in on the right hand and cleanse the left hand, and vice versa, and if they want they can touch it to their foreheads to clear their third eye. As each person does this say: 'May this water purify your body.' The towel can be passed around behind the bowl or taken around by someone else.

When every person is done, wander around the outside behind everyone, sprinkling to cleanse the space. Make sure when the offerings go around to libate the kernips into the earth.

Anointing

Within our coven we only usually use anointing when we are performing initiation rituals, but it is a lovely step to use.

An anointing potion can be as simple as salt/blessed water, but it can also be an essential oil blend of your choosing, which can be created with an intent in mind such as protection or it can be made to honour a particular deity.

It can be used purely as a dab on the forehead or wrists and given with a few words asking for a blessing or protection.

The Great Rite

This is perhaps something with more of a Wiccan/ceremonial flavour to it, but useful to know about in case you want to incorporate it.

The Great Rite is the union between male and female, between the God and the Goddess and usually symbolically enacted by placing the blade of the athame into the chalice or a wand into a cup...it is symbolic...you get the drift.

It has been performed physically in some groups with the act of sex between the High Priest and High Priestess, but this is usually when they are in a relationship and most definitely consensual. As far as I know is not practised so much anymore... I could be wrong, perhaps I just don't get invited to those rituals...

It is an act to symbolise union, love, manifestation, creation and fertility, not just the pitter patter of tiny feet, but the fertility of all things. It is the interaction between male and female, yin and yang and all the energies uniting.

In some witchcraft traditions, the High Priest holds the athame as the male energy and the symbol of the God and the High Priestess would hold the chalice as the female energy and the symbol of the Goddess. However, this isn't always possible because not all covens have a High Priest and a High Priestess (ours has two High Priestesses!) and in a solitary ritual by defin-ition there is only one of you so any two people or one person can perform the task.

Words of insight can be said while performing the great rite (in its symbolic form, I dare say while performing it physically your mind is on other things...) Often the God and the Goddess will connect and pass on their wisdom or the Priest/ess can say a blessing or poem.

The chalice should have water or wine inside, the athame can be held in the air while the chant/words are said and then placed inside the chalice. It can be dipped in three times and then raised in the air or used to draw a pentacle. Tap the blade on the side of the chalice and then drink. If you are in a group ritual the chalice can be passed around the circle for all to drink from. An offering to the earth should be made either before or after drinking from the chalice.

Five-Fold Kiss

The five-fold kiss is often used as part of some Wiccan rituals, usually in initiations. A pattern of kisses is applied to the person by the High Priest/ess usually male to female or female to male. There are several different versions, but basically you kiss both feet, both knees and the genitals or sometimes the feet, knees, genitals, breasts and lips, forming a pentagram shape. Each kiss is accompanied by a blessing.

Blessed be thy feet, that have brought thee in these ways
Blessed be thy knees, that shall kneel at the sacred altar
Blessed be thy womb/phallus, without which we would not be
Blessed be thy breasts, formed in beauty/strength
Blessed be thy lips, that shall utter the Sacred Names.

Drawing Down the Moon

I have talked about this in more detail in my book *Pagan Portals: Moon Magic,* but it is a traditional ritual where the energy from the Moon can be drawn down into the Priestess (or Priest). The energy can be channelled through the person or you can use the blade of an athame or water in a cauldron to 'catch' and hold the lunar energy. If the athame is placed into the water you then combine the energy of the female Moon and the male athame, the water can then be drunk to absorb that power.

The same ritual can be worked in the day time to harness the powers of the Sun.

Raising Energy

Connecting with the energies of the ritual space for me is a must. When I am working in my house or garden I already have that connection, a kind of umbilical cord attached because it is my home and is full with my own energy and all the residue of magic that I have worked there. However, when I am outside in a field, a forest or another place, I like to connect with the energy of that place before I work a ritual. Close your eyes and put out your mental feelers…see what energy you can pick up. If the space has trees, plants or buildings then try to connect spiritually with them. Once you have connected with that energy source, it really helps when you need to raise the energy required for your ritual purpose.

Raising energy might be done by dancing, singing, chanting, playing drums. You can do whatever works best for you. In a group you can raise amazing energy by walking deosil (clockwise) around the circle banging drums or chanting.

Chanting

Chanting is an excellent way to raise energy and can be very effective in both solitary and group rituals. It only needs to be a short chant repeated over and over until you feel the right amount of energy has been raised (in a group ritual the High Priest/ess will signal when the time is right to release and stop chanting). There are plenty of pagan songs with catchy words that can be used. Another interesting way to raise energy with words is to play the 'word association' game going around the circle. The first person might start with the word 'drum' the next person quickly says whatever comes into their head first for instance 'beat' and the next person has to respond and so on…going around the circle as quickly as you can.

The Awen

In a druidic ritual the Awen is a lovely chant that is performed by all the members in circle and can be incredibly powerful. All members chant the word Awen over and over usually either three, six or nine times, but it is drawn out into three vowels so the word actually becomes; 'Aaaaaaaahhhhhhhhhhhooooooohhhh wwwweee eeennnnnnn.' (Difficult to type but you get the idea). Awen symbolizes the creative spark of inspiration and it is depicted as three dots with three rays of light leading down from them encompassing the importance of three – the three worlds (earth, sky, sea), three levels of druidry (bard, ovate, druid) and the triads.

Cone of Power

Cone of power is a term used for the energy raised in ritual. Basically once you create the energy you increase it until it comes to a peak, once it does you release it and send it out into the universe to do whatever you have asked of it. It is called a cone of power because that is the shape it forms as it is rising. The power starts slowly and builds gradually until the pressure is intense, then you release it. However you raise that energy, whether it is singing, chanting, drumming or whatever, you must remember to keep focused on your intent. In a group ritual it is usually the High Priest or Priestess who controls the energy and signals when to release it. Don't hold onto the energy once it is ready otherwise it will fizzle out like a damp squib; you need to release it when it is at its peak like an explosion of a firework. To give the power a good final send off the phrase 'So mote it be' is often said, accompanied by everyone throwing their arms into the air sending the energy on its way.

God and Goddess Positions

Sounds vaguely rude...it is not. The Goddess position can be used when evoking the feminine into the circle by standing with your feet slightly apart and both arms in the air in a Y shape. The God position can be used when evoking the masculine into the circle by standing with your feet together and your arms crossed over your heart. Both are often used after releasing the cone of power; the Goddess position first, then the words, 'So mote it be,' followed by the God position.

The Working

This is the part in your ritual when you do what you set it all up for, it might be working a spell, doing some healing, making an amulet or medicine pouch, psychic or spirit work, consecrating and charging tools or crystals or to connect with a deity in meditation, but it might also be just to celebrate the sabbat or the season or work with a particular Moon phase.

Divination

During a ritual is a fabulous time to work with divination especially if you are at a Full Moon. Any form of divination works; tarot, scrying, runes, ogham, whatever is your personal favourite. With the added boost from the elements and deity, it can be a powerful and enlightening experience.

Meditation

Sometimes it is nice to sit in ritual and do a meditation. If you are in a group, someone would read one out or if they are clever clogs will recite one from memory while everyone follows quietly. If you are solitary, it is a nice time to just sit and connect with the deities you have invited to join you or allow your mind to wander…

Offerings

I always think it is nice to give an offering when in ritual, it may just be in the form of leaving some wine and crumbs on the ground for the animals or as a thank-you to Mother Earth, but you can also make specific offerings or blessings after your ritual working, it is only good manners. You may want to just say a blessing or read a poem to the deity you asked for help or guidance from, but you might also want to leave a physical offering such as some nuts, honey, fruit or something natural like a pentacle shaped from straw or twigs. You can get your creative ideas flowing for this one, but please make sure it is biodegradable and not dangerous if animals come and investigate. We often leave a little star-shaped salt dough with a tiny crystal inside at the foot of one of the trees in the grove that we hold our rituals in.

The Feast

It wouldn't be a book of mine without the mention of cake... Feasting in the form of breaking bread or cake to share is done in a lot of group rituals; it is symbolic of the male and female energies as well as being good for grounding your energies. Usually some of the wine and cake are put onto the ground as an offering to the God and Goddess that have joined you in ritual. Quite often everyone will drink from the same cup, which is passed around person to person. When the drink and food are passed around the phrases, 'May you never hunger,' or, 'May you never thirst,' are often stated on offering the food or drink. The recipient then answers with, 'Blessed Be.' In more formal rituals the members of the circle come up to the altar to be served.

The word libation is used a lot in this situation, what it actually means is 'a drink poured out as an offering to a deity'. The recipient will take the cup and make a statement (silently or out loud) usually to give thanks to deity, to honour ancestors or to give general thanks, then they pour a little onto the ground or if indoors pour it into a bowl (mind the carpet). Then they will take a sip. We also break a little of the cake or bread and sprinkle that on the ground, usually under a tree so that the animals can find it.

Traditionally wine or mead are used, but we often have children in our groups or those that don't drink, so we tend to have soft drinks which we match to the purpose of the ritual. When we held a ritual to honour the element of fire we all drank cinnamon tea, for instance. And in the cold winter months we tend to serve hot chocolate to keep everyone warm rather than wine. If you do serve wine and you have youngsters or non-drinkers, they can just 'inhale' the scent of the wine instead.

It is more usual to have bread to break and share, which is symbolic especially during the harvest months, but we do like our cake so that's what we do. We make homemade cakes for everyone to share. And in fact at a recent hand fasting Tracey made heart-shaped shortbread cookies for the couple to break.

Endings

Thank Deity

It is very important to thank deity for joining you in ritual; it is after all only good manners to do so. Thank them for their presence, for lending their energy to the ritual, for their support and guidance and bid them farewell. Technically if we invoked or evoked deity at the start now we must work a devocation or sending away/off or, as we affectionately refer to it in our coven, 'bugger offs'. It is a way of releasing the energies that have joined you in ritual, just remember to be respectful and polite, you are thanking them and saying goodbye not dismissing them as if they were of no consequence.

Often the words, 'Hail and farewell,' are used but also, 'Farewell and blessed be.'

Different examples of deity bugger offs can be found in the ritual examples section of this book.

Release the Elements/Quarters

Then you must thank the elements and bid them on their way. If you have called in elementals or Guardians it is important to thank them properly and send them on their way. You don't want them hanging around after ritual as they might cause some mischief!

Releasing the quarters is done in the reverse order to that used to invite them. You turn and face the direction you wish to say farewell to, thank them for their presence and bid them on their way. If you have used candles at the quarters, blow the candle out after releasing each element.

You can see some examples of releasing the quarter calls in the ritual suggestions part of this book.

Close the Circle

This is done in a similar way to the casting, but you walk widder-shins (anti-clockwise) around the circle, 'undoing' the circle that you cast. Visualise the light dissipating and dissolving away.

Don't forget to ground and also, if you are outside, please make sure to check you haven't left any rubbish behind...

Ritual Planning

Beasts and Birds

You probably won't associate animals with rituals unless you are referring to sacrificing them; this isn't about that particular subject unless you are working a Voudou ritual that requires a cockerel… What I am referring to are pets such as cats and dogs. There are various trains of thought on this subject (as always). If you have a pet that works as your familiar then obviously you will want them in ritual with you. Cats especially like to get involved (or should that be interfere?) in all things magical. But some people are of the opinion that animals in a circle can be disruptive and that nothing should cross the boundaries of a circle once it has been cast. I am going to say this again…go with what works for you.

We have had lots of fabulous open rituals in our local forest where people have brought their dogs with them, some of the dogs sit under the trees quietly, and some of them even sit in circle with no worries. Where we hold our open rituals we also get passersby and their dogs are always crossing our circle…but that may be to get to the cake. At a recent hand fasting we also had an audience of horses.

Having a Laugh

I have attended rituals where I was required to keep a very straight face and be extremely serious, I struggle with that…a lot. It actually makes the ritual very uncomfortable and un-enjoyable for me, but that's just my personal opinion. When we write and organise our open rituals we make a lot of effort to get them right, but on the day it doesn't always work out perfectly, we are human after all.

People make mistakes, the weather likes to make an appearance and all sorts of other outside influences happen… Oh and my wicked sense of humour really does get in the way. When you work with the mischievous crowd that I do, who like to put totally unpronounceable deity names in the script, it doesn't help. And, of course, once you have fallen over a word it will keep repeating...during one particular ritual I said 'elephants' instead of elements and I just couldn't shake it. In another ritual the mere mention of the deity Gong Gong produced a rousing chorus of the camp fire song 'Ging gang goolie'...and don't even get me started on the sniggers that occur when the 'Horned God' is mentioned...

I like to think that the Gods have a sense of humour and I like everyone in circle to feel comfortable, happy and relaxed, for me that comes in the form of not worrying about being strict or too serious in ritual. Each to their own, you may prefer it another way.

Got a Question?

We are a teaching coven; we like to run a ritual where people feel comfortable in asking questions as we go along about what we are doing. Some groups prefer people to ask questions before or after the ritual but not during, just check before you enter the circle.

Scripts

I have worked rituals without a script and I have worked impromptu on the spot rituals in the middle of nowhere with no tools or pre planning, but as I have a brain like a sieve I prefer to work with a planned outline and a script, especially if I am leading an open ritual as it helps the whole event to run more smoothly. In most of the rituals I have attended the people leading have had scripts or notes of some sort, so it is OK to use them. No one will frown upon you for not having remembered all 15 pages of words...it also helps for those people calling quarters that are a bit nervous, they definitely prefer to have something to read out rather than having to make it up on the spot or remember it all. But as I am sure my lot will tell you...I have a habit of going 'off script' anyway...

Quick at-a-Glance Guide

1. Cleanse yourself and the ritual space
2. Cast a circle
3. Call the quarters
4. Invite deity
5. Raise energy
6. Do spell work
7. Give offerings
8. Feast and drink
9. Thank deity
10. Release the quarters
11. Close the circle
12. Ground yourself

Do I Need a Reason?

Rituals can be held for any reason. The more traditional ones are to celebrate the turning of the wheel and the sabbats, that includes rites of passage, to recognize the seasons, for spell work of any kind, to meditate, to work with particular deities or, as we have done before with our coven, to work with the elements or a particular intent (such as prosperity). You also don't need to do the whole thing; a simple circle can be cast on its own without all the rest of the whistles and bells. Just cast a circle to bring protection for psychic or spirit work, to meditate or to bring you some inner peace and calm.

Part 2

May We Present To You a Host of Rituals...

In this section of the book I would like to share with you some suggested ritual scripts. The first section is on rites of passage with explanations about each one and ritual examples, and then we have some sabbat ritual scripts followed by some random ritual ideas just because we love them and some of those are scripts from open rituals we have held as Kitchen Witch. Huge thanks to my Kitchen Witch co-High Priestess Tracey Roberts and our lovely coven Hearth Guardians Samantha Leaver, Sue Perryman, Vanessa Armstrong, Stacey Mantle and Joshua Petchey for allowing me to share their writings.

Rites of Passage

Within the pagan world there are several different rites of passage, as there are in many cultures around the world, I would like to share my view of the main ones with you.

Most rites of passage rituals are led by a celebrant; this is usually someone who has earned/gained the title of High Priest/ess or Arch Druid.

Dedication

If you have chosen to walk the path of witchcraft (or druidry, or any pathway at all really) you may want to do a self-dedication. I did this myself many years ago just as a way of making a commitment not only to the Gods, but also to myself. It doesn't have to be anything complicated and you can incorporate as much bling, trimmings and ceremonial doo dahs as you want to.

You are dedicating yourself to show your commitment to your chosen pathway (although they do tend to twist and turn along the way) and to the divine. You may choose to wait until you have been studying for a year and a day or you may want to make this your first ritual, it is your choice. A New Moon is a good phase to perform a self-dedication on as it has the energies of new beginnings. This is not an airy fairy decision to make; it takes some serious thought before you declare your dedication.

Start by grounding yourself then, when you are ready, sprinkle some salt on the floor and stand on it (it doesn't need to be much, just a pinch will do). Or if you prefer a bit more of a ceremony you can cast a circle, call in the quarters and deity.

Then light a white candle in front of you and look at the flame. Think about why you are doing this ritual, why are you choosing to dedicate, and what it means to you.

Then speak; you can sit beforehand and write some self-dedication words or you can go with the flow and say it from the heart (or wing it as I call it).

Ask for a blessing from the Gods; ask that they allow you to seek their wisdom and guidance along your path. State that you will always treat them with honour and respect and that you will follow their guidance to the best of your ability. If you want to you could use the fivefold kiss blessing at this point, but anoint yourself (rather than someone else doing it as self-dedications are usually solitary affairs).

If you have chosen a specific path or pantheon to follow/work with, then state your pledge of loyalty at this point too.

You can bless and dedicate a piece of jewellery as well. I used a pentacle pendant.

Then just sit quietly for a while in meditation in case they have any insight for you.

When you are ready give thanks and extinguish the candle.

If you cast a circle and called in the quarters and deity, you will need to release them too.

Initiation

If you belong to a coven at some point you may wish to be initiated; it is a big deal and a huge honour (to you and to your coven) and a commitment. Not only do you pledge yourself, your loyalty and your support to the coven, but also to every member within it...so make sure you have thought it through.

Some covens require you to have completed your first level of training with them before you initiate, some don't. Some druid groups will initiate you at the beginning of your training and it varies between groups and traditions.

It is a big step on your spiritual journey and not a decision for everyone.

With our coven, one of the High Priestesses leads the initiates off from the main circle and through a yew tree grove as a symbolic journey from their old life through one of death and rebirth (the magical energy of the yew tree) and back to the circle.

Then we ask them if they are willing to pledge their pathway to that of a witch, to learn the craft of the wise, its lore, symbols, rituals and mysteries, sharing their experiences good or bad with each other and exploring with an open mind and open heart. We ask them to devote themselves to following the ways of the witch, the Kitchen Witch Coven and the Gods. At which point, hopefully, the initiate answers yes.

Tracey and I (both the High Priestesses of the Kitchen Witch Coven) give a pledge in return to the initiate that we will teach all we know, guide and support and answer any questions to the best of our ability.

We then perform an anointing ceremony where the third eye is anointed to help them see truly in this world and the next, the throat so that they may speak truly and receive the truth and the hands so that they may heal others and themselves.

We then present the initiate to each of the quarters to ask for witness to the pledge and blessings associated with that element. North brings strength, stability and reflection. East brings thought, wisdom and clarity of vision. South brings passion, change and transformation and west brings healing and guidance with their emotions.

We finish with a statement:

From this day forth, you will walk hand in hand and in the love of the God and the Goddess as a walker of the old ways and Priestess/Priest of the Kitchen Witch School.

Wiccaning/Naming Ceremony

I held Wiccaning/naming ceremonies for both my children when they were about a year old.

Particularly with my first child, I wanted a beautiful blessing as I had had a horrible pregnancy and all sorts of complications with the birth, so the beautiful experience I anticipated turned into a bit of a nightmare. The naming ceremony was in part my way of moving on from the bad experience of the birth.

There are many emotions involved from finding out you are pregnant to giving birth and then a whole heap of new ones while children grow up; some good, some wonderful, some not so good. Celebration of life really starts once a person becomes pregnant, the anticipation and excitement, the planning and preparing both physically and mentally. Rituals and spells can be worked during this time to ask for safe labour and protection during pregnancy and childbirth.

In the druid tradition new babies that are born are giving a rite of welcoming, often combined with a naming rite at which the child is given a name and where the parents choose guardians or God/Goddess parents. This is when they make their vows to honour and care for the child.

A Wiccaning or naming ceremony can be a small private event with just the parents and the child or a grand affair, or anything in between. Witches and pagans who have Wiccanings for their children use this ceremony to formally announce the child's name to the community to invoke protection for the child and to ask the community to teach the child the values that are important to them. Also at this time deity can be called upon to bless the child.

The most popular age for a Wiccaning seems to be between birth and one year. Although as I understand it a Wiccaning can be performed at any age, even adults – perhaps if they wish to change their name or at a point of rebirth for themselves.

I don't think it matters where the ritual is held – in a house, in a garden, a field, or the woods – wherever the parents feel comfortable.

Wherever the ritual is to be held, the area should be blessed, cleansed and consecrated beforehand. Perhaps request permission from the spirits of the place to accept the ritual and add their energy to it to help make the day run smoothly.

Create a sacred space, maybe decorated with flowers and foliage. Cast the circle, but with the allowance that people and/or children may run or walk in or out, especially if they are not pagan and don't understand circles.

A formal ritual may just include the parents and the child inside, or perhaps a less formal situation with everyone sitting around in a circle. I think it helps to have an altar as a focal point. It doesn't have to be anything grand, but may be decorated with flowers again and contain all the tools and essentials for the ritual.

A celebrant leads the ritual, holds the energy and ensures that the ritual flows properly. If you want a less formal event, a parent or family member could say the words.

The ceremony can be very flexible. But a basic guideline would be:

1. Everyone gathers around the circle.
2. The child and the parents stand at the circle's edge.
3. The celebrant bids a welcome and gives an outline of what will happen.
4. The circle is cast.
5. The celebrant calls the spirits/elements/guardians/ quarters – whatever suits the parents' beliefs.
6. The circle is cast.
7. If deities are to be called this would be done too.
8. The celebrant then speaks a little about the glory of birth, or new life, of the changes that happen within the family. The celebrant might now ask the parents to hold hands and vow their love to each other and their guardianship of the child.
9. Then the celebrant asks the God/Goddess parents to step forward and make their vow to the child.
10. The child is blessed by the elements, the deities or spirits. Maybe even taken to each direction and held up.

11. The child is then given her name in sight of deity.
12. Thanks is given to everyone, then the quarters are released, deity thanked and the circle uncast.

I don't believe Wiccanings are historical because 'Wiccan' is a fairly modern term, but I do believe our ancestors held naming ceremonies or blessing ceremonies for new babies. Perhaps something simple such as holding the infant up under the stars and asking blessings from deity.

A Naming Ceremony by Vanessa Armstrong

I set up an altar with the following:

White candle for purity, spirituality, truth and peace.
Blue lace agate crystal for protection particularly for children (or mother of pearl , an infant/newborn protection crystal).
An incense burner with a blend of sandalwood and jasmine incense for clearing negative energy and promoting peace and serenity. Each person in circle can also be smudged with this incense.
A chalice filled with Full Moon water for the blessing.

The naming ceremony is held outside if it is a nice day. Guests stand in the circle, with the parents and child inside it near the altar.

Cast the circle, saying the following:

As we gather in this place
Hand in hand, we connect
Our energy – happy and pure
This circle it will protect.

Call the elements, saying:

Element of earth, we call upon you in this naming
To help this child with stability and growth
To feel the connection to you from his/her feet
May you nurture him/her as they grow
Hail and welcome!

Element of air, we call upon you in this naming
To show this child communication and inspiration
To breathe in deeply and feel your caress on his/her face
May you power their mind and intellect as they grow
Hail and welcome!

Element of fire, we call upon you in this naming
To show this child energy and passion for life
To feel your warmth and observe your power
May you bless him/her with drive and vision as they grow
Hail and welcome!

Element of water, we call upon you in this naming
To show this child the feeling of friendship
To feel your healing and cleansing waters
May you bless him/her with purity and compassion as they
grow
Hail and welcome!

When we have asked the elements for their blessings, the parents
or/and guardians may want to say a few words themselves as to
what they wish for their child as he or she grows up.

Taking a few drops of the Full Moon water from the chalice,
the High Priest or Priestess or the person conducting the naming
ceremony anoints the child on his/her third eye and in doing so,
says:

Element of spirit,

Bless this child with potential and of promise.
Whose path is just beginning and is unknown.
May your divine knowledge ignite this spark of new life
Guide him/her on their forever continuing journey through
life.
Blessed be!

There may be guardians of the child appointed and they could perhaps say a few words. Gifts for the child may also be presented at this time.

When all is spoken and gifts presented, it is time to thank the elements and to close the circle. Say:

Element of water, we thank you for your presence in this naming
For showing us compassion, clarity and friendship
Hail and farewell!

Element of fire, we thank you for your presence in this naming
For showing us to be passionate for life, your energy and your warmth
Hail and farewell!

Element of air, we thank you for your presence in this naming
For showing us inspiration and our ability to communicate
Hail and farewell!

Element of earth, we thank you for your presence in this naming
For showing us stability and freedom to grow.
Hail and farewell!

As our hands were joined

And now we disconnect
Our hearts and minds are still as one
This child we still protect
Blessed be!

Menarche (Female)

This is the point in life when a girl becomes a woman, when she begins menstruation. I have never seen this part of life as 'a curse' as some call it. Even when I have had bad ones, to me it is a part of the cycle of life; it is part of what makes me a woman.

Menstruation can start as young as 10, it can be as late as 17 or anywhere in between. Traditionally this was seen as a celebration of life, but in modern times it has become a subject described as a curse or a nuisance.

However, the Jewish culture still recognises the event. The Ghanaian people celebrate this event with a party; South African Gwi people decorate the young woman with patterns.

A girl from the Sioux people would have a purification ritual and guidance from a holy woman. Some cultures involve piercing as part of the ceremony.

The menarche rituals I have researched involve gathering all the women within your community to celebrate. A lot have no men, though, or girls who have not begun menstruation, yet they sometimes attend. They are invited to congratulate the new woman at the end of the ritual and give her gifts.

An idea for this ritual would be to create sacred space.

Perhaps have an altar with symbols that are relevant; a picture of the Earth, deity statues, pictures of honoured family members and flowers. A flower garland for the girl to wear would be good too.

Cleanse and consecrate the space as you would normally.

The ritual could include dancing and singing to celebrate.

The girl could choose a Moon Mother to attend the ritual with them, to hold her hand and reassure her.

A Moon Father could be chosen to 'crown' the girl after the ceremony with a circlet of flowers.

The girl should be dressed in white and anointed with sacred water. Then she should be led into the circle where everyone is already chanting and raising energy. The girl would then turn and call out their name, symbolising leaving the girl child that they were behind, leave the circle and change into a red dress or perhaps just put a red sash on.

Meanwhile all the other women in the circle could pass round a talking stick; as each one receives it they should speak two or three words that summarise their own menarche experience.

The girl re-enters the circle and more singing and celebrating follows.

The Moon Mother would then bless her and perhaps give her a new 'Moon name'.

Then if men have been excluded they could join the group and the celebrations. Maybe there could be some storytelling and drumming too.

Coming of Age (Male)

I believe the coming of age to be very important. It is a time in a lot of cultures when a child becomes an adult. The magical age for boys seems to be 13.

Thirteen is quite a special number, it is a number of transition. 'One' is the individual person starting on the divine path, 'three' is the number of faces of the Goddess (or perhaps for Christians the holy trinity). Numerology adds all the numbers together until there is only one, so 1+3=4; four is the number of the whole or the full circle of life.

This age would possibly be a good time to talk to a child about procreation and sexuality. I do believe it is a good idea to be honest and open out such things. I would rather a child learns the correct details about a parent and be able to ask questions than learn the perhaps misunderstood details in the playground!

The Jewish community marks this occasion with a celebration. Native Americans, Africans, aboriginal tribes all mark the occasion of a boy becoming a man. However, it doesn't seem to be something that we do in Europe or America from what I can tell. Some cultures involve piercing or tattooing as part of the ceremony.

Perhaps a gift would be nice, maybe some grooming products?

As for a coming of age ceremony I would suggest a similar ritual to that of a Wiccaning.

Hand Fasting

A hand fasting is a pagan 'wedding' based on ancient Celtic traditions.

Historically a hand fasting was seen as a rite of betrothal lasting a year and a day. If the relationship went well the couple would then hold a second hand fasting ceremony that would bind them together as long as their love was shared.

This custom spanned the centuries and was still legal in many parts until 1753 when Lord Hardwick passed an Act through Parliament declaring that marriages in England could only be legal if sanctioned by the Church. This law, however, was exempt in both Scotland and the Channel Islands. The Act set the precedence for modern Church marriages in the UK ever since with some updates being allowed for modern times. However, hand fastings continued to be legal in Scotland up until 1939, and were particularly used in the Highlands and Islands where they may not have had a permanent clergyman. If this was the case, a hand fasting ritual could be performed, then when a travelling clergyman visited the community the marriage could then be carried out by the Church. As a direct result of Lord Hardwick's Act and its strict marriage laws, the famous town of Gretna Green became popular with English couples running away to get married, as Scotland was outside the jurisdiction of English law.

Hand fastings today usually go straight to the second ceremony. A hand fasting can last forever, as long as the love is still there, even into future lives.

The setting for most hand fastings seems to be outside in a natural place close to the elements. The space is usually decorated with flowers and foliage. The ceremony is presided over by a High Priest or High Priestess who the couple chooses. The space is made sacred and the quarters/elements are called.

The couple are invited into the sacred space to exchange vows with each other. As they give their promises to each other, the celebrant binds their wrists together with a cord. This is the actual 'fasting' part signifying their love and knots that indicate their bondage of mutual commitment. This is probably where the saying 'tying the knot' comes from. Rings can also be exchanged at this point. At a lovely hand fasting that I had the honour of being a part of, we started with four elemental hand fasting ribbons that I tied around the wrists of the couple. Then we had a whole heap of different coloured ribbons for members of the circle to come and tie on as well, allowing them to also give their individual blessings to the couple.

When the ceremony is over the couple jump the broomstick. This symbolises the joining together of man with woman, to ensure their future happiness and love.

I have read about what was called the 'besom wedding', an unofficial custom that was considered quite lawful in parts of Wales until recent times. A birch besom was placed aslant in the open doorway of the house, with its head on the doorstep and the top of its handle on the doorpost. First a young man jumped over it, then his bride, in the presence of witnesses. If either touched or knocked it in any way, the marriage was not recognised. In this kind of marriage, a woman kept her own home and did not become the property of her husband. It was a partnership, 'cyd-fydio' rather than an ownership. A child of the marriage was considered to be legitimate. If the couple decided to divorce, they simply jumped back over the broomstick again, but this could only be done in the first year of marriage. If a child had come, it was the father's responsibility.

Traditionally hand fasting cords were red in colour, which symbolised desire, vitality and passion of love.

One custom is, while facing each other, the couple place their right hands together and then their left hands together to form an infinity symbol while a cord is tied around their hands in a knot. Another custom is that the man and woman place their right hands only together while a cord is used to tie a knot around their wrists.

Going back through history, records were not kept for who got engaged, married, had children and died. Today the sacraments of the Church have the responsibility of taking care of these things. Before the Church took over these duties, these things were overseen by the whole community and therefore were set in law by their witnessing what happened between the couple making the promise.

If a hand fasting was performed with the two left hands together without the tying of the knot, as was the custom of rich and influential German nobility, it meant that the woman was a mistress and would not be able to claim the name, inheritance, property, etc. of the real wife and was only in the protection of the man. But her offspring would be taken care of as legal heirs second in line to the man's legal and first wife. Having lots of children was once the only form of 'social security' in one's old age.

Hand Fasting Ritual

We were very honoured to lead a hand fasting ritual in a beautiful forest setting for one of our lovely coven members Esther and her beau Geoff. This is the ritual we used. As they work specifically with the Norse Gods we incorporated that into the ritual script. The ritual was led by myself and Tracey as High

Priestesses of the Kitchen Witch Coven. The quarters were called by friends of the couple and deity was invited in by two of our coven members.

Small altars or markers were placed at each of the four directions and a small altar table set in the edge of the circle. We chose to put the altar at the north edge of the circle rather than in the centre so that people could see what was going on and so that we would not have our backs to anyone.

An entrance or gateway into the circle was marked out at the east; there just happened to be two very conveniently placed trees in the east edge of the circle forming a natural gateway.

Casting the circle

Tracey walks deosil around the circle scattering rose petals to make the outer circle as she walks.

Rachel:

As I cast the circle round, feel the energy abound
Energies of old arise, our energies joined, this ring's comprised
A web of love, a web of light, to weave our ritual tight
A ring of earth, light from the sky, Runic rhymes and energy high

Within this circle we shall call, elements comprising all
That none may enter here within, and protection from without
Within this circle, hand to hand, between the worlds we now stand
This circle is now cast, all within from first to last

Calling the quarters

Liz:

Spirits of the east, spirits of the air

Ravens of Odin
Bring to us purification and clarity
Your thought, memory and all seeing
Spirits of air, welcome and blessed be!

Chris:

Spirits of the south, spirits of the flame
Wild boar of Freyr
Bring to us your creativity and passion
Your glow, light and force
Spirits of the flame, welcome and blessed be!

Mark:

Spirits of the west, spirits of the water
Horse of Odin
Bring to us your deepest intuition and truest emotions
Your strength, power and world walking
Spirits of the water, welcome and blessed be!

Claire:

Guardians of the north, spirits of the earth
Wolves of Odin
Bring to us your spirit of prosperity
Your leadership, vision and companionship
Spirits of the earth, welcome and blessed be!

Inviting deity

Ness and Laurine:

Hail Thor, Lord of the hammer
Lord of the storm that tears across the sky
Plain speaking, protector, bringer of clarity
Hail and welcome!

Hail to Sif, golden wife of thunder
Queen of the hall, peace weaver
Cup bearer and Goddess of kith and kin
Hail and welcome!

Hail Odin, Lord of Asgard
Warrior, valiant and wise
Protector and bringer of wisdom
Hail and welcome!

Hail Frigga, all knowing Queen
Protector, peace weaver
Bringer of discretion and prudence
Hail and welcome!

Hail Frey, lord of the fields
Lord of the Vanir, bringing riches of heart and hearth
Lord of love that is bound to the land
Hail and welcome!

Hail Freya, great Goddess of the Vanir
Mistress of magic and art of seeing
Shape shift our lives to embrace your mysteries
Hail and welcome!

Rachel:

We call upon the deities Thor and Sif, Odin and Frigga
and Frey and Freya
Grant your blessing and protection upon these two,
who have come before you,
to celebrate the sacrament of marriage
in the presence of their friends and family.

With abiding faith in you, and continuing faith in each
other,
they will pledge their love today.
May their lives always bear witness to the reality of
that love.
So mote it be.

Rachel:

This lovely ritual has its roots in ancient times and many believe that it developed in the Celtic cultures of Europe and the British Isles.

Originally it was a betrothal or a promise of marriage between two people who would then spend a traditional term of a year and day together to see if they were compatible. After this time, and if they were in agreement the vows could be taken again and they would be considered married.

The hand fasting ritual takes its name from the joining and tying of the hands of the couple to be wed, usually with cords. This is where the term 'tying the knot' comes from today in reference to getting married. The hand fasting ritual would have been performed by an important member of the community – chieftain, Priest, Priestess, Shaman or Elder, who would have guided the couple through the ritual and presided over them as they exchanged vows in front of witnesses, probably the whole community. The witnessing of the ritual by friends and the community would make it law in the eyes of the community as no official records would have been kept until the introduction of a 'Church-based' wedding.

Today, hand fasting is the choice of many Pagans and magical folk when choosing to commit to a partner.

For those that are not familiar with Pagan practices I will explain what we are doing as we go along, but please if anyone has any questions just ask…

Tracey:

And now we shall introduce Esther and Geoff to the elemental powers to seek their blessings.

Bride and groom walk to the east.

They say:

>Hail, winds of the east!

Liz (Standing, holding incense, facing the couple):

>What is it you seek from the powers of air?

Esther:

>We seek your blessing and guidance for our marriage.

Liz (while wafting incense towards them):

>Blessed be your marriage with these gifts from the east:
>Clear understanding of each other, and of yourselves.
>Knowledge that each day is a fresh start of your life as a couple.
>Joy in learning and growing together.

Liz then hands the bride a yellow ribbon, motions the party onward, and sits down.
The couple moves to the south.

They say:

>Hail, fires of the south!

Chris (standing, raising a candle, facing the couple):

>What is it you seek from the powers of fire?

Geoff:

>We seek your blessing and guidance for our marriage.

Chris hands the couple the lit candle to hold together.

Chris:

>Blessed be your marriage with these gifts from the south:
>Shared discoveries and experiencing new things together.
>Inspiration to find new ways to surprise one another.
>Opportunities to take on new ventures, and receive great rewards, together.

Chris collects the candle from the couple, replaces it on the altar, hands the bride a red ribbon, motions the party onward, and sits down.

The couple moves to the west

They say:

Hail, waters of the west!

Mark (standing, raising a shell of water, facing the couple):

What is it you seek from the powers of water?

Esther:

We seek your blessing and guidance for our marriage.

Mark (sprinkling water on the couple):

Blessed be your marriage with these gifts from the west:

Clear understanding of each other's desire.

Resolve to stand by each other, no matter what may come to pass.

Patience in those moments when needed.

Mark then replaces the shell on altar, hands the bride a blue ribbon, motions the party onward and sits down.

The couple moves on to the north.

They say:

Hail, land of the north!

Claire (standing, raising small bowl of earth, facing the couple):

What is it you seek from the powers of earth?

Geoff:

We seek your blessing and guidance for our marriage.

Claire:

Then each give me your hand.

Claire then sprinkles a little bit of earth on the backs of the bride's and groom's hands.

Claire:

Blessed be your marriage with these gifts from the north:

Strength to do what you must do, when you must do it, and together as one. Fertility, in all its many forms and manifestations.

Stability, such that you can always meet each other's needs.

Claire replaces the bowl of earth onto the altar, hands the bride a green ribbon, motions the party onward and sits down. The bride and groom then take their places at the high altar.

Tracey:

Love is an integral part of life, for without the spark of love, there is nothing to empower the mystery of continuance and without continuance, and all life will cease to be. This is how we came to be, and now we are gathered here together because our parents, and our parent's parents, and so on before them, felt that spark, and empowered that continuance, and made it possible for us to be who we have become.

So it is today that, in the presence of the people, in the power of the Ancients, in the abiding love of the Lord and Lady, Esther and Geoff are about to marry one another, and share that spark of love with one another, and perhaps in this moment we too will feel its energy and again participate in that mystery of continuance that becomes life itself.

Please join hands with your betrothed.

Above you are the stars, below you is the land, as time passes, remember...

Like a stone should your love be firm, like a star should your love be constant. Let the powers of the mind and of the intellect guide you in your marriage, let the strength of your wills bind you together, let the power of love and desire make you happy, and the strength of your dedication make you inseparable. Be close, but not too close. Possess one another, yet be understanding. Have patience with one another, for storms may come, but they will pass quickly.

Be free in giving affection and warmth. Have no fear and let not the ways of the unenlightened give you unease.

The bride and groom say their vows to each other. First Geoff then Esther (they wrote their own personal vows).

Rachel:

Geoff, I have not the right to bind you to Esther, only you have this right. If it be your wish, say so at this time and place your ring in her hand.

Geoff:

It is my wish.

Rachel:

Esther, if it is your wish for Geoff to be bound to you, place the ring on his finger.

The bride places a ring on the groom's left ring finger.

Rachel:

Esther, I have not the right to bind you to Geoff only you have this right. If it is your wish, say so at this time and place your ring in his hand.

Esther:

It is my wish.

Rachel:

Geoff, if it is your wish for Esther to be bound to you, place the ring on her finger.

The groom places a ring on the bride's left ring finger.

Geoff:

> I, Geoff Breeze, in the names of the Lord and Lady that reside in us all, and in the love that resides within my heart, take you and you alone, Esther Spelman, to be my wife and beloved partner.
>
> I promise that I will honour our union with words of adoration and actions of consideration, and I commit myself to work together with you, and to grow with you, as individuals and as a family.

Esther:

> I, Esther Spelman, in the names of the Lord and Lady that reside in us all, and in the love that resides within my heart, take you and you alone, Geoff Breeze, to be my husband and beloved partner. I promise to bring to our union my compassion, understanding, fairness, and unconditional love. I commit myself to honour, respect, believe in, and grow with you, through the many challenges that lie before us.

Rachel:

> The hand fasting knot, which binds two lovers' hands together, represents their sincere and hopeful intention to make a solid union. Each of us has our own thoughts on the matter, our own words to say, our own hopes and blessings.
>
> In a moment, I will invite you all to come and add to the knot of hand fasting. But first, we will start with the bride's and groom's ribbons, which represent the good things that each brings to share in marriage.

The bride and groom join their left hands, Rachel ties their hands together with the elemental ribbons.

Rachel:

> Now I invite the people to come and join the bride and

groom, and offer their blessings and wishes to them. As each of us contributes our ribbon to the knot, we share with Esther and Geoff our love, friendship, and support for the marriage they are making. Bound together around their hands, the ribbons demonstrate our collective support of their decision to marry one another.

Guests come and tie their ribbons around the couple's hands, offering such blessings and wishes as they may.

Rachel:

Now raise your hands together, so that all may see.

The bride and groom raise their hands.

Rachel:

Made to measure, wrought to bind, blessed be, these lives entwined!

By the powers vested in me by the Goddess and by the Elders of our faith, I now pronounce you husband and wife. You may kiss now...

What you have here done together with one another, let no one break apart.

May the Lord and Lady take notice of, and be favourably inclined toward your union, and may you be blessed with health, prosperity and fruitfulness, from this day forth and forevermore. So mote it be!

I present to the people here assembled, and to the Gods and the spirits of this place, Esther and Geoff.

Tracey:

And now, as in all marriages, you have certain duties towards each other.

She pours wine from a decanter into her cup, and passes the cup into the bride and groom's left hands, which are bound together. She then takes up the athame from the altar and passes it into the bride and groom's right hands, above the cup.

Bride and groom:
> As the athame is to the lover, so is the cup to the beloved.

The bride and groom lower the athame into the cup, saying:

> And conjoint, they bring blessedness.

Tracey then pours from her cup, one-third each into both the bride's cup and the groom's cup. Then she gives the respective cups into the couple's free hands.

Rachel:
> This is your first drink together. May you never thirst!

The bride holds the cup for the groom while he drinks, then the groom holds the cup for the bride while she drinks; then the Priestess returns both cups to the altar.
Tracey breaks the biscuit, offering a part to the Gods and giving a piece each to the bride and groom.

Rachel:
> This is your first food together. May you never hunger!

The groom holds the biscuit for the bride while she eats. The bride holds the biscuit for the groom while he eats.
A personal blessing is read out by a friend of the couple.
A besom is then placed down on the ground about in front of the main altar. The besom is held in place by volunteers.

Rachel:

This will be your first leap of faith together.

The couple jump the broom and join the guests.

Thanking deity

Ness and Laurine:

Thor, Lord of the hammer
Lord of the storm that tears across the sky
We thank you for your presence here today
Hail and farewell!

Hail to Sif, golden wife of thunder
Queen of the hall, peace weaver
We thank you for your presence here today
Hail and farewell!

Hail Odin, Lord of Asgard
Warrior, valiant and wise
We thank you for your presence here today
Hail and farewell!

Hail Frigga, all knowing Queen
Protector, peace weaver
We thank you for your presence here today
Hail and farewell!

Hail Frey, lord of the fields
Lord of the Vanir, bringing riches of heart and hearth
We thank you for your presence here today
Hail and farewell!

Hail Freya, great Goddess of the Vanir
Mistress of magic and art of seeing

We thank you for your presence here today
Hail and farewell!

Thanking the elements

Claire:

Guardians of the north, wolves of Odin
We thank you for your protection and aid
We bid you hail and farewell!

Mark:

Guardians of the west, horse of Odin
We thank you for your protection and aid
We bid you hail and farewell!

Chris:

Guardians of the south, wild boar of Freyr
We thank you for your protection and aid
We bid you hail and farewell!

Liz:

Spirits of the east ravens of Odin
We thank you for your protection and aid
We bid you hail and farewell!

Unwinding the circle:

Tracey walks widdershins round the circle.

Rachel:

As the strands of the circle unwind, this circle is open
but never broken
Merry meet, merry part, merry meet again!

Hand Parting

A hand parting is a Pagan divorce, a way to dissolve a hand fasting that has been made in honour of the fact that sometimes people do grow apart over time.

Unlike a divorce, unless the couple has also chosen to follow the laws of the land and have a registered marriage license and certificate, the binding agreement is between the two parties and the God and Goddess. To undo a hand fasting, you must go to the location where it took place (if this is possible). It is not necessary to invite the gathering, just the person who officiated the hand fasting and do a reversal on the ceremony, known as a hand parting, to set free each individual from the binding and let each go their separate ways in goodness and love.

A simpler idea is a 'cutting the cords' kind of ceremony. To do this, visualise the connections between you both, and ask which ones are appropriate for the relationship you wish to have now. Leave those, and cut the others. You might leave a strong connection at the heart and decide to sever the rest at least temporarily, allowing the ones that need to be there for your friendship to grow back.

Croning

I love the idea of a croning ceremony.

The word crone is derived from the word *'cronus'* (time) and it means the wisdom gained through lifelong experiences. Krone also means crown. To become crowned crone then acknowledges that you are a wise woman who has gathered up the fruits of her experience into profound and sovereign understanding. The wise crone becomes the resource of wisdom for her community and a source of inspiration for her circle of cronies.

A croning ceremony acknowledges the transition into a crone or wise woman, usually when a woman has gone through menopause. The last menstruation is a farewell to the motherhood stage of a woman's life. A doorway is now open to step through into the crone phase. Media would have us believe that staying young and firm is what it's all about. Although I am not at the crone stage yet I do have grey hairs (you can't see them as I use hair dye) and I am starting to get wrinkles and my body is already fighting against gravity. I am not necessarily happy with all these changes, but I do intend to welcome and celebrate my crone stage when it arrives.

This passage celebrates the end of the time that our energies are turned outwards toward physical activities and marks the beginning of the time that we turn our energies inwards, toward more spiritual activities. Our physical growth slows down, and gradually our physical bodies begin to separate from our spiritual bodies.

In some cultures now and in the past when a woman has gone through the menopause she keeps her wise blood inside her and it increases her wisdom. Elder women were and should still be revered and honoured. A croning ceremony provides acknowledgement and celebration of this.

This can be a personal ceremony, or held with a few close friends or a big celebratory party.

A croning ceremony may include creating sacred space and having all your friends participate. The Priest or Priestess could say a few words about the person, her qualities and traits. Then each guest could share some memories or mementos.

Then the Priest or Priestess could say a few words about life and its various stages, how each stage marks changes in our lives and each stage adds to our characters. The person could then be crowned with a circle of flowers.

A presentation of three stones could be made to represent her life – past, present and future.

A candle is lit to represent the light of wisdom; salt is given to represent eternal wisdom and experience and a re-dedication to deity can take place if desired.

Croning Ritual by Rachel Patterson

I have written this ceremony with myself in mind (when the time comes) so I have used my matron and patron deities and references to my spirit/totem animals.

Decorate the altar with a Cailleach statue and a Ganesha

statue (my matron and patron deities), rocks and crystals, autumnal leaves and orange, red and yellow flowers.

Casting the circle

Walking deosil (clockwise) around the circle, sprinkling leaves to create the boundary and say:

As I cast the circle round about to keep unwanted energy out
Bring in the fresh new beginnings energy of the maiden
Bring in the powerful passionate energy of the mother
Bring in the strength and wisdom of the crone
This circle is now cast

Calling the quarters

To the element of earth and the direction of north
I invite you to join our rite and bring with you
Your powers of stability, grounding and family ties
Spirits of the earth, spirit of the dragon
Welcome and blessed be!

To the element of air and the direction of east
I invite you to join our rite and to bring with you
Your powers of intellect, intuition and clarity
Spirits of the air, spirit of the magpie and pigeon
Welcome and blessed be!

To the element of fire and the direction of south
I invite you to join our rite and bring with you
Your powers of creativity, passion and transformation
Spirits of the fire, spirit of the wild boar
Welcome and blessed be!

To the element of water and the direction of west
I invite you to join our rite and bring with you

Your powers of seeing beyond the veil and the flowing of emotion
Spirits of the water, spirit of the frog and the seagull
Welcome and blessed be!

Inviting deity

Hail, The Cailleach, old and wise one, she of the winter, the snow and ice.
Who rules over death, wisdom and the weather.
Join us today and remind us of the cycles of life, encourage us to face our fears and show us strength and courage.
Cailleach, hail and welcome!

Hail, Ganesha, Lord Ganapati, elephant headed God of success, knowledge and prosperity and destroyer of obstacles.
Join us today and bring your strength and passion and bring your spiritual guidance.
Ganesha, hail and welcome!

Work

Ask all those present to work around person to person and just say something about how they feel about the crone aspect.

A good friend will say a few words at this point – about the 'new' crone. Her characteristics and personality – I suspect there will be some embarrassing stories at this point...

Then back around the circle again, ask everyone to share a memory that we have shared, or perhaps a photograph of us.

Then an appointed friend will say, as she places a circle of flowers on the new crone's head:

Throughout life we pass through many stages. Each stage marks and brings about profound change in our lives – birth, education, leaving home, marriage, children – all bring significant change and identity to our lives. This crowning announces, and in many respects, creates the stage or state of sovereignty in your life.

At this stage in your life your focus will shift from the exterior world of conventions to the freedom of being the ruler of your own inner realms. Your challenge is to make known your understanding of life and lend your wisdom to enlighten others to life's beauty and beyond, its light and shadow. For the awakened woman holds the keys to sovereignty as ruler of her own life.

The circle of the crown is a symbol of the Sun and of the Earth and the universe. A circle for love that never ends, a circle for arms that embrace. A symbol of friendship, for friendship breaks down all boundaries and has by its very nature to be a circular flow of giving and receiving.

The circle is a symbol of unity into which your life is joined in an unbroken circle to those whom you choose to love and befriend, so wherever you go in life, your love will constantly be returning to them.

Then she places a hand over a small pouch containing three crystals, saying:

These stones represent your life – past, present and future. One represents your past; one the present; and the other the future. It does not matter which is which, for we are all inter-connected, all in process – from rock and shell to stone and sand. One grain of sand makes a whole beach. Time is both her-story, and potential happening, in this one moment – always in the now.

Love, friendship and wisdom are formed through shared experiences and these experiences are refined by the purity of the fire of your feelings. These glass stones are sand refined by fire. They represent that love, friendship, and wisdom has substance as well as soul, a present as well as a past.

The experiences you have had together, through confidences shared, through joy, fun and laughter, and despite occasional sorrows, have polished your love, friendship and wisdom into a closeness that shines with good memories and gives a sparkle not only to today, but to your futures together.

However painful the past, you have learnt much wisdom from it; however much you have had to struggle, there have been rich days like today; however daunting or hopeful the future, your experiences, expectations, learnt knowledge and feelings have shaped and will carry on shaping and developing your own unique wisdom.

And so today, among the people gathered here, you have entered a new stage on your journey through life. Now you can look forward to new ways, to the untapped energy within you that you have yet to discover, the undiscovered opportunities, joys and challenges.

May you receive wisdom and courage to take hold of the rest of your life and live it to the full. Fulfil your dormant ambitions, discover new talents and find the time and space to enjoy your life.

So mote it be!

Releasing the quarters

To the west and water, spirit of the frog and seagull
We thank you for your presence today and bid you hail and farewell!

To the south and fire, spirit of the wild boar.
We thank you for your presence today and bid you hail and farewell!

To the east and air, spirit of the magpie and pigeon.
We thank you for your presence today and bid you hail and

farewell!

To the north and earth, spirit of the dragon.
We thank you for your presence today and bid you hail and farewell!

Thanking deity

Ganesha, Lord Ganapati we thank you for your presence here today, for your guidance and assistance in all things.
We bid you farewell for now, until we meet again.
Remain in our hearts, watch over us and guide our feet along the pathway that is best for us.
Farewell and blessed be!

Cailleach, we thank you for the secrets you have shown to us, for the strength and wisdom you have given.
We bid you farewell for now, until we meet again.
Remain in our hearts, watch over us and guide our feet along the pathway that is best for us.
Farewell and blessed be!

Unwinding the circle

As the circle unwinds, as the threads unweave, we hold peace and love in our hearts.
This circle is open but never broken.
Merry meet, merry part and merry meet again.

Sage Hood

During my research I also discovered a similar ceremony for men that reach 'elder hood' or 'sage hood'. It was also traditional to gift a man on reaching elder hood his staff. It seems the traditional cloak or cape is presented at croning or elder hood. Sometimes both are referred to as sages.

I also found a lovely idea for once you reach crone hood or

elder hood. Set aside a certain time each week to sit and meditate. For that meditation you take yourself to the world of spirit (the Otherworld not the alcoholic sort). Go on a short journey at first to see where it takes you, then on each visit go further and find yourself a home in the spirit world, each future journey you add to it and make it your own. Each week re-examine the details you have made previously and add to them. This meditation creates your very own perfect place ready for when you cross over.

Crossing Over

A crossing over or passing over ritual is a way of honouring a departed loved one, of giving blessings and thanks for their lives and honouring their memory. It can also signify aiding their spirit to move on. We all have to pass through the veil at the end of each lifetime. It is this final passage that is celebrated.

Our belief in the Old Religion is the eternal cycle of birth, death and rebirth. The spirit never dies, but when physical death occurs the spirit moves to another world where it continues to exist until it is reborn again into another physical life.

A ceremony could include creating sacred space and calling the quarters. These could be offerings on the altar for the God and Goddess of the underworld. A candle on the altar represents the spirit of that person, lit at the beginning of the ritual.

A few words can be said about the person who has passed over, to honour their memory, by the Priest or Priestess; maybe going around the circle and asking each person to add a few words too. As each person says their words, they could sprinkle some flower petals into a cauldron filled with water in the centre of the circle.

The Priest or Priestess then asks all the elements to guide the person on their journey. Then deity is asked to guide and protect the person to the Summerlands.

When the Priest or Priestess feels the loved one has departed, they snuff out the candle. They wrap the candle in silk, spoon some of the water and petals from the cauldron into a holder and present both items to the person who requested the ritual for their loved one. Although sometimes it is preferred that the candle should be left to burn out on its own.

A memorial rite can also be performed after a 'mainstream' funeral. This ritual calls upon the deceased in order to complete any unfinished business in the material world, and to bid a final farewell before sending the spirit to Summerland.

Wheel of the Year

A lot of pagans (not all) will celebrate the sabbats; these mark certain seasonal events in the year. Some were most likely celebrated by our ancestors, but some are newer additions to the pagan calendar.

Yule – The Winter Solstice

Around 21st December it is the rebirth of the Sun and the longest night of the year, but from this point forward the power of the Sun begins to grow.

Imbolc

Usually 2nd February it is the festival of lights looking forward to the beginning of spring and the lighter days.

Ostara – Vernal Equinox

Around 21st/22nd March this is the spring equinox when Mother Earth awakens.

Beltane

Usually 1st May this is a fiery celebration and is all about ooh la la and va va voom, the beginning of the birds and the bees creating baby birds and bees.

Litha – Midsummer – Summer Solstice

Around 21st June it is when the Sun is at the peak of his power and the day being the longest of the year. The celebrations are for summer and the abundance of Mother Earth.

Lughnassadh/Lammas

Usually 1st August this is the celebration of the first harvest.

Mabon – Autumn Equinox

Around 21st September, Mabon is a more modern name for the autumn equinox and celebrates the second harvest, it is the end of the growing season and the beginning of autumn.

Samhain

Usually 31st October it marks the beginning of the Celtic New Year, the last of the harvest is collected and stored and the veil between the worlds is thin, it is a time to be thankful and to remember those that have gone before us.

Saturnalia Ritual by Samantha Leaver

(17th – 23rd December approximately)

'Io Saturnalia!' Two thousand years ago this was the seasonal greeting that would have chimed out across most of Europe, not 'Merry Christmas'.

Originally a one-day harvest feast at the end of autumn, Saturnalia gradually moved to later and later dates, with longer celebrations throughout the Roman period.

For seven days from the 17th December it was party season in Roman times. A lengthy mid-winter period of merry-making and the season of goodwill. Saturnalia was the Roman festival of misrule in honour of the agricultural and harvest God Saturn.

During this festival, there was a reversal of traditional roles with slaves wearing fine garments and sitting at the head of the table for at least one banquet. Homes were decorated with wreathes and greenery. Wax tapers and torches were lit – in a similar way to advent candles.

Gambling was allowed and the festival is described as a joyful period. Over-eating, gambling, drinking, singing and sharing witty tales were all part of Saturnalia celebrations. Those who did not join in were considered scrooges and humbugs.

The Sigillaria – held on the 23rd December was a day of

present-giving in Ancient Rome.

Apollonius Sophistes created a beautiful ritual which used the themes of autumn/winter – storage/preparation, the pleas of the winter solstice for plenty and abundance in the new light and of course the honouring of the harvest God Saturn. It is a wonderful winter solstice/Saturnalia 'mash-up' and is a strong example of how ancient celebrations can be adapted into the modern world. Here is an example of this ritual modified again for solitary use.

It honours Saturn (God of Harvest), Consus (God of Storage) and Ops (Goddess of Plenty and Saturn's wife and sister). Three single-day festivals within the Saturnalia season are named after these deities and therefore this ritual compresses them into one ritual – Consualia, Saturnalia and Opalia.

According to Sophistes, the sources for this ritual are Macrobius' *Saturnalia* (Bk. I, Chs. 7, 8, 10 and 11) and Scullards' *Festivals of the Roman Republic* (pp.205-7).

Tools you will need

A Father Christmas figurine or Saturn statue (place in a glass bowl)

A Mrs Claus Figurine or Ops statue

Candles – tea-lights work well and plenty of them

Some sunflower or corn oil

An oil burner

Some string/yarn/wool/thread in appropriate festive colours

Play dough or air-drying clay

Cookies and sweets – those chocolate gold coins are FAB!

Some festive coloured cloth

A treasure chest – some sort of box, a hamper basket would be lovely

Uncooked oats or uncracked grain such as barley

Pennies – shiny ones if possible

Pot of earth (in place of doing the ritual outside if you can't)

Santa hat – to wear of course throughout the ritual and festivities

Before the ritual preparation

If the Father Christmas figurine hasn't been used to represent Saturn before, bind his feet together with thread and consecrate it through incense of frankincense. Then tie loose bows around him for decoration. If the figure has been used before it will continue to carry the energy of Saturn so just do the decorations.

Make some oval shaped cookies and decorate them with simple faces. Wrap the cookies and chocolate coins/sweets in cloth into a flat package and place them in the bottom of the treasure chest or hamper.

Make Sigillaria – flat oval clay faces similar to the cookies. Make a hole for hanging in each one, so that later, for Dionysia, they can be hung on a pine tree.

Prepare a feast – this is a good time to get the pigs in blankets, stuffing balls and Brussels sprouts out. YUM!

Location: Do it outside! Otherwise use the pot of earth.
Timing: 17th December, 21st December or 25th December.

What to do

Right before the ritual open your treasure chest/hamper and your pantry/food cupboards. Give thanks for the stores (corresponds to Consualia, which happens before Saturnalia).

Walk to your shrine/sacred place and shout 'Bona Saturnalia!'

Cast your circle as you would normally or use the following example words:

We circle round creating sacred space,
Invoking from the Heavens' holy grace.
We call the Gods to guard our solemn rite,
And ward this hallowed ground with walls of light.

Let sky above and earth below unite,
A bond established by Olympic might.
Let fear and discord leave without a trace,
And peace prevail within this holy place.
Let word be deed in this decree.
As it said, so must it be!

Tell the Universe why you are here

Welcome to Saturnalia! The circle of the year is cut in fourths, and in the ancient lands of Greece and Rome the darkening time from autumn equinox to winter solstice was the time to plough and plant the ground, to store away the seeds. When this was done the people rested through the winter months, until the Sun returned. Three ancient Gods are honoured at this time: Saturn, Ops, and Consus are their names.

You can read the myth of Saturn to yourself or as a group, recite it for everyone.

Slowly fill the bowl your Father Christmas is sitting in, then say:

When Saturn rules, all things are turned around, and everything becomes its opposite. Just once each year this figure is filled up; it's empty while Saturn lies asleep. We feed him with oil that's been pressed from corn (or similar), the golden nectar from the nuggets born. So also we in wisdom store away our energy to use another day. Drink deep Saturn, of this golden oil! Return our gift and bless our sacred soil!

Open the hamper/treasure chest and say:

Saturn has an aid, the God of Storage, who guards the seed corn; Consus is his name, which means to hide things, mostly underground. We open up the secret storage chest and place the seed corn safely into it. From what we have reaped, we always save a bit, uneaten, using it to seed new growth. A portion of our hard-won money too, we put away to use another day. And even some of our best thoughts are hid, to later bring to light when they can grow. All this and more is hidden in the earth, committed to the care of Mother Ops. Remember all the bounty you have reaped; consider what it is wise to save inside.

Circle the sacred space clockwise, each time you come to the open treasure chest/hamper sprinkle some but not all of the grain and coins into it.

While you circle chant:

Save the seed corn for sewing; plant the seed to start it growing.

Sit back down in front of the altar and rest, then say:

But now your weary work is almost done; commit to Consus all the rest you hold.

Place the treasure either on the ground if you're outside or near the pot of earth.

Take a candle and Sigillaria (clay face). Move the face sunwise around the altar/shrine and say:

Let me pass the gifts around the sacred circle, moving like the Sun. Since ancient times these gifts have been exchanged: the waxen candles, calling forth the Sun, the little figures, symbols of our souls, these inexpensive gifts have been decreed by Saturn so that no one will feel poor.

Light the candle – if you do this in a group, you can light the candle to the left of you so there is a chain of candles being lit, or if you're on your own light your own candle and then light each candle on your shrine/altar. Say:

Now as the Earth revolves around the Sun, we pass the light around the circle thus, and as each year the light returns to us, the candle flame comes round to bring rebirth. The lights remind us how Saturn led us from the murky night of ignorance, and freed us from the dismal darkness of starvation, to the light of the wiser ways.

When the candles are all lit place the Sigillaria into the earth pot. Say:

In dedicating symbols of our souls, we dedicate ourselves to Saturn's work.

Pour the oil from the bowl around Santa into an oil lamp and say:

Saturn brings the Sun's bright golden light that wakens hidden seeds to come to life. The seed is nourished in the fertile earth by Saturn's wife the Queen of plenty, Ops.

Light the oil or the candle underneath it and say:

This time of year we loosen Saturn's bonds. The ancient God awakens from his sleep and rules the Earth as in the Golden Age.

Circle the altar/shrine. Say:

Bring light to wake the seed: let the shoot from earth be freed!

Continue circling and chanting, untie the woollen bows around Santa. Say:

Saturn, Ancient Father, hear our prayer. As we untie your woollen bonds this year so let the hidden seeds be brought to birth and let your Golden Age return to Earth.
Io Saturnalia! Io Saturnalia! Io Saturnalia!

Magic the cookies and other treats from the hamper so it looks like you have put the seeds and coins in and been given treats in exchange (children love this). Say:

Behold the gift of Saturn! See his work! Behold how seed and money are transformed! And see how carefully saved and hidden seeds become fruits that satisfy our needs. I taste the fragrant fruit a gift from Saturn and his wife Ops. I will share some with people near me for that's the law in Saturn's Golden Age.

Touch the earth and say a prayer of thanks before munching on cookies and treats.
Say a formal thanks to Saturn, Ops and Consus:

You gracious Gods: Saturn, Consus and Ops, accept my thanks and look on me with love. Thank you for allowing me to see that seed/corn and wealth must be saved, that I need the light to bring my seeds to fruit. As I have done this day, so every day!

End the rite by saying:

The rite is ended. Io Saturnalia! Io Saturnalia! Io Saturnalia!

In a group setting you would have baked a bean into one of the cookies; the person who gets the bean is the Lord or Lady of Misrule and will lead the drinking and eating that comes next. If you are on your own, get feasting, drinking and watch a silly festive film.

At the end of all of the festivities rebind the legs of the Santa figure and place it away for next year. Keep the seeds, money and a candle as a reminder of the returning light.

Imbolc Ritual by Sue Perryman

Decorate your altar with symbols of Imbolc: pots of early spring flowers such as snowdrops, crocus, daffodils etc., Brighid's cross, lots of candles and a cauldron together with a drink of wine, milk or juice and something to eat (biscuit or cake).

Colours: White, orange and red

Incense: Frankincense, rosemary, myrrh or cinnamon

You will also need a small plant pot, some compost, a few seeds of your choice, a small jug of water, a pen and small square of paper. It is a good idea to have a small bowl of water and a small towel to wash and dry your hands with too.

Light the candles and incense and sit before your altar for a few minutes thinking about the meaning of Imbolc, your life and plans for the future.

Ground and centre.

Sweep the circle.

Walk around the circle three times repeating the chant below or one of your own while directing the energy with whatever tool you usually use to cast a circle (wand, athame, sword, finger).

From the deep dark forests
To the oceans and the seas
From the parched arid deserts
To the wind blowing free
Protect this circle so mote it be.

Face the east and say:

> Spirits of the east
> You bring the fresh spring breezes, and the strength of the hurricane
> You are spring, new beginnings, intellect and our thoughts
> I ask you to watch over me and lend me your energies for my circle this day
> Hail and welcome!

Face the south and say:

> Spirits of the south
> You bring warming fire to our hearths, and the rage of the volcano
> You are summer, passion and energy
> I ask you to watch over me and lend me your energies for my circle this day
> Hail and welcome!

Face the west and say:

> Spirits of the west
> You bring the cleansing rains and the ebb and flow of the tides
> You are autumn, healing and our emotions and dreams
> I ask that you watch over me and lend me your energies for my circle this day
> Hail and welcome!

Face the north and say:

> Spirits of the north
> You are the fertile soil and the planet Earth, our home
> You are winter, stability and fertility

I ask that you watch over me and lend me your energies for
my circle this day
Hail and welcome!

Face your altar and say:

Brighid of the healing waters and sacred flame
I call you and your consort, the Lord of the Wild
To join me in my Imbolc ritual if you will
And to watch over and protect me
Hail and welcome!

Smudge yourself and your circle with the incense then stand
again before your altar and say or read to yourself:

Imbolc is also known as Candlemas or Brigid's day
(pronounced Breed). It is one of the Celtic fire festivals and
celebrates the very first signs of spring. Snowdrops and
crocuses rear their heads above the frozen ground and below
in the dark earth other plants are stirring. The first lambs are
born at this time of year and the most common explanation of
Imbolc is 'in the belly', which refers to the pregnant ewes.

At Imbolc the Goddess returns as maiden and the God
who was born at Yule is now a young man. Imbolc is the time
of year for purification, re-birth and new beginnings. It is the
festival of Brigid. She is a Goddess of healing, poetry and the
hearth, childbirth and smith craft and is associated with fire,
springs and wells.

Think about what goal you would like to bring into your life and
write it on the square of paper, fold it in half and put it into the
bottom of the plant pot. Fill almost to the top with compost. Hold
a couple of seeds in your hands and visualise yourself achieving
your goal and charge the seeds with your dream. Gently push

the seeds just under a thin layer of compost and water them lightly. As the seed grows so will your goal. Don't read anything into it if it doesn't grow – it can happen for a variety of reasons and doesn't mean you won't achieve your goal eventually.

Eat and drink, saving a small portion of both as an offering to the deities/spirits.

When you are ready face the north and say:

Spirits of north, thank you for watching over me and lending me your energies.
Hail and farewell.

Turn to the west and say:

Spirits of the west, thank you for watching over me and lending me your energies.
Hail and farewell.

Turn to the south and say:

Spirits of the south, thank you for watching over me and lending me your energies.
Hail and farewell.

Turn to the east and say:

Spirits of the east, thank you for watching over me and lending me your energies.
Hail and farewell.

Turn to your altar and say:

Brigid and the Lord of the Wild.
I thank you for joining with me for my Imbolc ritual and for

watching over and protecting me. Stay if you will, go if you must.

Walk widdershins around the circle repeating:

The circle is open but never broken.

Ground and don't forget to take your offering outside for the deities/spirits.

Ostara Ritual by Tracey Roberts

Items needed
Besom
Dried herbs or flower petals to cast the circle
Plant pot or a plastic cup
Soil
A whole egg
Seeds (something that reminds you of the Sun, daisies, marigolds or sunflowers. Or something that you will use, maybe tomato or lavender)
Water
Cake or biscuit (obviously)
Wine or juice

Start the ritual by sweeping the circle and ritual space. Visualise negativity leaving as grey dust and being replaced by positive white light.

Casting the circle
Cast your circle walking deosil (clockwise) and sprinkle with herbs or dried flower petals and say:

I cast this circle of sacred space

A boundary to hold balance and peace
My circle welcomes in the awakening land
In glowing thread of love and light, so mote it be.

Calling the quarters

Facing east say:

I call to the element of air, spirit of the sylph
Spirit of the hawk and skylark
Bring with you the soft spring breeze that awakens new life
I welcome you into my circle of balance and rebirth
Hail and welcome!

Facing south say:

I call to the element of fire, spirit of the salamander
Spirit of the serpent and dragon
Bring with you the strengthen Sun that awakens the land
I welcome you into my circle of balance and rebirth
Hail and welcome!

Facing west say:

I call to the element of water, spirit of the undine
Spirit of the salmon and mermaid
Bring with you the gentle rains of spring that awakens the
land
I welcome you into my circle of balance and rebirth
Hail and welcome!

Facing north say:

I call to the element of earth, spirit of the gnome

Spirit of the wolf and bear
Bring with you the fertile soil that awakens the land
I welcome you into my circle of balance and rebirth
Hail and welcome!

Invite deity

I call to Gaia, Mother Earth.
The land is once again awakening and I hear your call
I welcome you into my circle of balance and rebirth
Hail and welcome!

I call to the God of the greening land
I feel your spark of life return to the earth once more
I welcome you into my circle of balance and rebirth
Hail and welcome!

Work

Take a moment to draw up energy from the Earth while you are visualising what seeds and dreams you wish to plant in your life. What is it you want to nurture and bring into the world?

Still visualising your intent, put a layer of soil in the pot. Then place the egg in, whole. Visualise the egg yolk, a symbol of the Sun God wrapped in the embrace of the Mother Goddess symbolised by the egg white. Male and female energies in perfect balance.

Then take the seed or seeds and hold them in your palm. These are the potential of new life. Pour the energy you have drawn up from the Earth into the seed and then plant it in the soil.

Then say:

Gaia, Mother Earth. Bless these seeds of potential and help me to tend them and nurture them. With your love may they grow strong and healthy.

Cover the seeds with more soil if needed. Then water the pot. As you water, visualise the seed sprouting out through the soil. See just the little green shoot to begin with then as time goes on growing bigger and stronger and eventually with your love and careful nurturing see it as the full grown plant. Then set the plant down.

It's cake time! Eat and drink a little to ground the energy you have raised. Don't forget to give some to the land in thanks.

Releasing the deities and the quarters and closing the circle

Once you feel grounded, prepare to close your circle. Say:

God of the Greening Land.
Your spark of life has once again returned to warm the land and my heart
I thank you for lending your energy to my circle today
I bid you hail and farewell!

Gaia, Mother Earth
The land has once again awakened in answer to your call
I thank you for lending your energy to my circle today
I bid you hail and farewell!

I thank the element of earth, spirit of the gnome
Spirit of the wolf and bear
Your fertile soil will nourish the seeds of my hopes and dreams
I thank you for lending your energy to my circle today
I bid you hail and farewell!

I thank the element of water, spirit of the undine
Spirit of the salmon and mermaid
Your gentle spring rains will nourish the seeds of my hopes

and dreams
I thank you for lending your energy to my circle today
I bid you hail and farewell!

I thank the element of fire, spirit of the salamander
Spirit of the serpent and dragon
The warmth of your strengthening Sun will nourish the seeds
of my hopes and dreams
I thank you for lending your energy to my circle today
I bid you hail and farewell!

I thank the element of air, spirit of the sylph
Spirit of the hawk and skylark
Your soft spring breeze will breathe life into the seeds of my
hopes and dreams
I thank you for lending your energy to my circle today
I bid you hail and farewell!

Walk widdershins around the circle. Say:

I release the threads that bound this circle
Nothing but love now remains
Blessed be!

Beltane Ritual by Stacey Mantle

Colours: The deep plum of wine/grapes, gold for the returning
of our beautiful Sun; green for the lovely fields of grass; white for
the purity of love.

Items needed
One tea light candle for each person at the ritual
Ribbons in the above colours or the colours of your choice
that represent Beltane to you, about 12 inches in length

A stick of wood for a handle to secure the ribbons to (hopefully found loose on the ground). If you need to trim it from a tree, please make sure to ask its permission first.

For the altar

Cloth of gold
A shell to hold water for the west
A green candle for fire for the south
A few rocks and a bit of earth to represent north
Sandalwood incense for air for the east

Casting the circle

Walking deosil to open the circle, say:

As I walk our circle I sprinkle sea salted water to not only give us strength within, but also as a barrier in which we can be safe to join our forces and be successful in our work.

I cast this circle now one time, so Ancient Ones will hear my rhyme.
I cast this circle now times two, for hidden wonders and secret truths.
I cast this circle three times round, and now declare this sacred ground.

Calling the quarters

To the east, I call to thee fill my visions and set us free.
Share your strength build it strong that we may succeed in this day's throng.
Hail and welcome!

To the south I turn my gaze, bright the lights and clear the haze.
Strengthen our will, keep it sound that we may succeed all

around.
Hail and welcome!

To the west and water I turn to now feeling the spray upon my brow.
Clear our minds and help bend our ways. Stand strong with us and increase our stays that we will succeed in all our days.
Hail and welcome!

To the north I do now turn, for our mighty Earth will help us learn.
Bring us your will to see things through. Aid in our work and all that we do.
Help us find our dreams and make them come true.
Hail and welcome.

Calling the Goddess

Goddess beautiful Goddess true. Join us in honouring the Beltane fires through.
That we may join the throng of love and passion and bring our hearts together as one for the promises of the future have now begun.
Hail and welcome!

Calling the God

Great God we ask that you join with us in our Beltane rite.
We call to our fires, our passions and the light.
Stand with us and join us now, we honour you come be with us now.
Hail and welcome!

Introduction

Beltane is the festival of passion and a celebration of fertility, when the stag God races through the woods to join and marry our beautiful Goddess.

We join our hearts with the intent to call a bountiful harvest to come. We honour the Beltane fires not only calling the warmth and brightness of the Sun so desperately needed for the coming seasons, but for these beautiful fires to inspire our own passions – not only in love of one another but also our beautiful Earth. The animals mate and bring forth their young, our plants, trees and flowers share pollen and strengthen each other that we might continue to live on our beautiful planet.

Work

Gather your ribbons and your wooden sticks. Get a friend to hold the stick or hold it yourself and set it somewhere where you can make it secure. Secure each ribbon with a knot at the top of the wood, moving around the diameter of the stick. With each colour, as you begin to braid the ribbons, think over what you are passionate about: your sweetheart, your children, your families, your home, your garden and your work. Imagine the fires of Beltane rising higher and higher with each thought. You can braid all of the ribbons or do just part of them so that there is a 'tail' of free ones. I enjoy re-braiding mine each year and find that small children love to play with them. Honour your life, what you have accomplished thus far and that which you still intend to do. Set your goals and find ways to reach them. Let the rising flames of Beltane remain in your heart along with your passions. Say:

May this Maypole of Beltane be a constant reminder to us to continue to follow our passions, succeed in our goals and never give up.
Blessed be!

Releasing the God

Great God we thank you for your presence, love and passion.

We are grateful for you in our daily lives.
Hail and farewell!

Releasing the Goddess

Beautiful Goddess, thank you for joining us this day.
We honour you and strive to carry goodness in our hearts.
Hail and farewell!

Releasing the quarters

Spirit of the north, of mighty mountains, stag and bear.
We thank you for your presence this day.
Hail and farewell!

Spirit of the west, water so nourishing and refreshing.
Thank you for your presence this day.
Hail and farewell!

Spirit of the south, the mighty fire and heat.
Thank you for your presence this day.
Hail and farewell!

Spirit of the east, the breeze that clears the cobwebs from our
minds that we may realize our possibilities.
Thank you for your presence this day.
Hail and farewell!

Say thanks

To each and every one of you here this day for our blessed
Beltane ritual, thank you for your love and strength in our
work today. May we be ever mindful for all that we have in
our lives. May we go forth as the wheel turns and be of help
to those in need, share our love and passions and bring forth
positive feelings and work for our beautiful planet.

Blessed be!

Opening the circle
Walking widdershins, say:

I now open this circle. May the work we began this day carry in our hearts and minds through the summer months bringing us great bounty to sustain us through the cold winter months to come. May this circle be open, but never broken.
Blessed be!

Faery Midsummer Ritual by Rachel Patterson and Tracey Roberts

You will need
A copy of the meditation below
Fairy cakes

Casting the circle
Walk the circle deosil whilst blowing bubbles...
Say:

With faery magic from King and Queen
Faerie footsteps to create a dream
This circle is cast to open the realm between the worlds
So mote it be!

Invite the elements
We call upon the elemental gnomes,
To bring us their stability and might
To join us from the earth in this rite
Blessed be!

We call upon the elemental sylphs

To bring us their intellect and insight
To join us from the air in this rite
Blessed be!

We call upon the elemental salamanders
To bring us their passion and fiery light
To join us from the flames of fire in this rite
Blessed be!

We call upon the elemental undines
To bring us their intuition and emotional sight
To join us from the watery depths in this rite
Blessed be!

Inviting deity

Come join us Faery Queen
Let us dance and circle around
Queen Mab with your magical insight
We invite you onto sacred faery ground
Come join us on this night
Faery blessings and welcome!

Come join us Faery King
Let us laugh and chant
King Oberon with your magical ways
We invite you onto sacred faery ground
Come join us, come and play
Faery blessings and welcome!

Smudge the circle.

Reading

This is summer's height, midsummer, the longest day and the shortest night of the Earth's solar year. Here we celebrate the completion of the cycle that began at the winter solstice.

Solstice means 'standing of the Sun' and we can take a moment to stop, be still and look back at our own unique journey since the winter solstice. By celebrating our achievements and acknowledging our failures, we can make sense of our actions and understand what we can learn from them.

In the past, the summer solstice was an important occasion. People stayed up all night to watch the Sun come up at dawn and many people still follow this tradition. Midsummer's eve and midsummer's day were traditionally the time for carnivals and processions.

Summer solstice is the time to count our blessings, to celebrate our achievements and our ever-changing selves. It is a time to celebrate each other and to be the embodiment of goodwill and positive energy.

Meditation to meet the tree spirits

If you are outside and near a tree go and sit underneath it. If you are doing this by yourself, read the meditation through first and then visualise it while meditating. If you are leading this meditation for a group, you can read it out.

Focus on your breathing, taking deep breathes in and out...

Visualise a tree before you, it might be one that stands around in your area or it might be one you are familiar with, the choice is yours. Its shadow extends toward you, but doesn't quite touch you.

See it standing strong and full. Feel the grass beneath you and the fresh air around you.

The sunlight penetrates the branches of the tree and casts a soft haze around you.

As you look around you see that you are in a small glen frequented by flower faeries and tree spirits. In the distance is a high mountain. This is a sanctuary, a place where the real and the imagined meet. It is the intersection of the mortal world and the faerie realm.

The tree stands strong in the midst of the grove. As you look upon it you see its simple beauty and strength. With that thought, a soft breeze passes through, rustling the leaves in response. And for a moment you are sure the leaves rustled your name.

You gaze upon the tree and see shadows and movements – tiny flickering – along the branches and at its base. At first you think it must be squirrels or birds, but you are unable to see them.

As you take in the entire sight of this tree, the lines in the bark begin to change and shift. You can see soft gentle eyes peering out from the bark. You are no longer watching the tree; you are being watched by it.

There is a shadowy movement and a form steps out from the tree itself to stand in its own shadow. It shimmers and shifts with incredible beauty. Around it flicker several tiny lights and you know they must be faeries. Peering around from behind it, you see a tiny elfin face, shy but curious. Then the spirit speaks your name. The leaves of the tree rustle again.

As you look upon this being, pay attention to what you experience. Are there specific colours? Fragrances? Do you feel a touch or tingle on any part of the body? Is this tree spirit male or female? Remember that those of the faerie realm will often use a form they think you expect.

It begins to talk softly to you. It speaks of its purpose and what knowledge it holds. It tells you its role in nature and what role it could serve in your own life. It tells you of the mystery of the tree, and why this one is so important to you.

See this as a conversation between you and the tree. Don't force it. Let the communication flow naturally. Let this being tell you about itself. Let it tell you why it wants to work with you. Don't be afraid to ask questions.

The leaves rustle with a singing sound as this being speaks. You may see birds and other wildlife start to gather around you, these will be signs of greeting in the future.

The tree being holds its palms upward, and the shadow of the tree extends further outward, until you are encompassed by it. You feel the shadow, it brings love, protection and promise. And then the shadow withdraws.

As the shadow recedes the eyes of the tree spirit hold yours until the spirit is drawn back into the heart of the tree. You can see its form within the natural configuration of the tree itself and know that you will forever recognise it from this day forth. The leaves rustle once more, whispering your name and then they are still.

You remember all that you were told.

Slowly, gently come back to this reality, shake your arms and legs and wriggle your fingers and toes.

Feast with the fairy cakes, obviously...

Thanking deity

King of the Faeries, blessed was your presence in this rite
May you now return to Elphame until we meet again.
Blessed be.

Queen of the Faeries, blessed was your presence in this rite
May you now return to Elphame until we meet again.
Blessed be.

Release the elements

Guardians of the west, undines of the water
We give blessings for your presence here today
May you now return to your realms.
Blessed be.

Guardians of the south, salamanders of fire
We give blessings for your presence here today
May you now return to your realms.
Blessed be.

Guardians of the east, sylphs of air
We give blessings for your presence here today
May you now return to your realms.
Blessed be.

Guardians of the north, gnomes of the earth
We give blessings for your presence here today
May you now return to your realms.
Blessed be.

Thanks and circle opening

Walk the circle widdershins. Say:

We thank the Faerie Queen and King, we thank the
Elementals and the Fae, and all of you here today. This circle
is open but never broken, merry meet, merry part, merry meet
again.

Lammas/Lughnasadh Ritual by Sue Perryman

This ritual was written to be led by two High Priestesses, noted
as HPS1 and HPS2, but could be conducted by any member of
the circle.

You will need

Note pad and enough pens or pencils for everyone present
A cauldron on the altar
A loaf of homemade bread and a chalice or glass of juice, wine
or water
A besom

Dried rose petals, smudging stick or incense and salt

Ground and centre.

HPS1 sweeps the circle, then casts the circle walking round it three times sprinkling dried rose petals and chanting:

I cast this circle, to keep us safe from harm, three times the circles cast about, three times is the charm.

HPS2 walks to the eastern quarter and turns to face it and says:

I call on the guardian of the east, element of air, you whose gentle breeze scatters the seeds that will grow into food to nourish us.
Join us if you will and watch over our Lammas rites.
We wish you hail and welcome.

HPS1 walks to the southern quarter, turns to face it and says:

I call on the guardian of the south, element of fire, you who are the Sun that shines down and ripens our crops.
Join us if you will and watch over our Lammas rites.
We wish you hail and welcome.

HPS2 walks to the western quarter, turns to face it and says:

Guardian of the west, element of water, you who nourish our crops so that they in turn grow and nourish us.
Join us if you will and watch over our Lammas rites.
We wish you hail and welcome.

HPS1 walks to the northern quarter, turns to face it and says:

Guardian of the north, element of earth, you who are the very foundation that supports and grows our crops. Join us if you will and watch over our Lammas rites.

We wish you hail and welcome.

HPS1 walks to altar, raises her arms to the sky and says:

Lugh, Lord of the Sun and of the harvest. Mother Earth, whose body brings forth fertility and life.

Join us if you will and watch over us during our Lammas rites.

We wish you hail and welcome.

HPS1 walks around the circle smudging everyone with incense or a smudge stick and other Priestesses follow sprinkling salt. (This could also be performed by two people from the circle chosen beforehand.)

Someone is asked to hand out the pens and sheets of paper to everyone in the circle.

HPS2 says:

The wheel has turned once more and we are here to celebrate the festival of Lammas also known as Lughnasadh, the feast of the Celtic Sun God Lugh who was seen as the God of Light, whose spirit was the life of the growing corn. It is the time of the first harvest, the harvest of grains. It was especially important to our ancestors as everyone was expected to help with the work of bringing in the harvest before the autumn rains came and the harvest would make the difference between starvation and nourishment throughout the winter.

HPS1 says:

Lammas is strongly linked to sacrifice, the sacrifice of Lugh who gives his life for the harvest and will be reborn again with next year's new crops. It is also a time for personal sacrifice so I decided it would be a good idea for each one of us to sacrifice some of our time to helping someone or something in our communities. It could be by donating some food to your local food bank or even just spending a few minutes of your time to chat to an elderly neighbour, maybe even offer to do some shopping for them. There are lots of things that we could all do to help someone and I am sure you can all think of something, however small, that might make a difference to someone in need.

We will take a few minutes while you all have a think and write down on your paper what you propose to do. When you have done this, fold your piece of paper up and come forward to place it in the cauldron.

You have until Samhain to do this when the paper will be burnt.

Give everyone some time to do this. Maybe the HPSs could drum or start cutting up the loaf to indicate that people need to finish writing.

When everyone has finished, the HPSs walk around the circle giving small pieces of bread and a drink of water or juice to each person, saying; 'Blessed be.'

When everyone has eaten and sipped, **HPS2** says:

Lugh, Lord of the Sun, and Mother Earth, our foundation, thank you for watching over us during our rites and for giving us this wonderful harvest.

Stay if you will, go if you must, we wish you hail and farewell.

HPS1 walks to the north and says:

Guardian of the north, element of earth, thank you for watching over us during our rites.

Stay if you will, go if you must, we wish you hail and farewell.

HPS2 walks to the west and says:

Guardian of the west, element of water, thank you for watching over us during our rites.
Stay if you will, go if you must, we wish you hail and farewell.

HPS1 walks to the south and says:

Guardian of the south, element of fire, thank you for watching over us during our rites.
Stay if you will, go if you must, we wish you hail and farewell.

HPS2 walks over to the east and says:

Guardian of the east, element of air, thank you for watching over us during our rites.
Stay if you will, go if you must, we wish you hail and farewell.

HPS1 walks widdershins round the circle and then they both say:

The circle is open, but never broken.

Cake time...

Autumn Solstice (Mabon) Ritual by Rachel Patterson

Walking deosil around the circle, smiling at her sisters and brothers as she goes and scattering multi-coloured flower petals to form the circle, the Priestess leading the ritual says:

> In the days of autumn these beautiful flowers bring their own power, for protection and spiritual guidance we cast the petals in a circle round and about to draw magic in while keeping negative energy out. For a happy home and to bring passion and love, for success and to bring joy and happiness.
> This circle is now cast; as above, now so below.

Turning to the east, she raises her arms to the skies as she feels the fresh beginnings of an autumn breeze, listens to small animals rustling in the forest, the gentle sound of wind chimes and breathes in spicy incense and calls to the Guardians:

> Element of air, knowledge and wisdom I call, in this time of harvest, bless us with your gifts during the season of autumn. Hail and welcome!

Turning to the south, she raises her arms to the skies as she feels the heat of the bonfire and watches the flames of the candles and calls to the Guardians.

> Element of fire, I call, brighten up our days, may the golden light of harvest bring illumination and passion in many ways. Hail and welcome!

Turning to the west, she raises her arms to the skies as she hears the crash of waves and feels the drop of rain on her skin and calls to the Guardians.

> Element of water, come to this circle of ours, may the blessings

of the harvest wash over us; add love, peace and intuition in this place and time.
Hail and welcome!

Turning to the north, she raises her arms to the skies as she gazes at the beautiful trees, their leaves starting to turn, looks down at the ground and wriggles her toes in the soft brown soil and calls to the Guardians.

Element of earth, I call to complete the task, may the power of the harvest bestow strength and success that will surely last.
Hail and welcome!

Returning to centre, holding her arms in a wide welcome, taking a deep breath to invoke the Goddess and with reverence, she says:

Elen of the Ways, light of the land, on you we call, brighten up our souls in these golden days of fall.
Goddess of the forest and all creatures who live within, grant us illumination and courage, grace and wisdom. Join us in circle today.
Hail and welcome!

Returning to centre, holding her arms in a wide welcome, taking a deep breath to invoke the God and with reverence, she says:

Herne the Hunter and the Green Man, we invite you in and ask that you bring courage and power and teach us to be brave and strong.
Join us in circle today.
Hail and welcome!

The Priestess then gives a speech about the autumn equinox:

The autumn equinox is a magical time. You can see the leaves start to change on the trees; you can feel the coolness in the evening air and see the dew on the morning grass.

The wheel is turning and changes are on the way; the trees and plants are preparing for the coming season and bring us a beautiful array of colours. The season of the witch has begun.

It is a time of giving thanks to the earth for the bounty that she brings and a time to give thanks for all that we have. The summer is coming to an end and autumn is taking over in preparation for the darkness that follows. Life is slowing down, packing away and storing energy for the winter months.

She moves to the altar and stops for a moment to admire the altar decorations, which could include a cornucopia full to bursting with apples, grapes, corn, wheat, beautiful coloured autumn leaves, pumpkins and squashes. Orange, gold and dark green candles, and a vase of autumn flowers.

She turns and faces centre, then turns slowly round to smile at everyone present, saying:

We gather today to experience the Crystal Grove. We will travel through the Forest where we whisper our desires, down to the Shore where we set our wishes free, then into the Ocean where we are cleansed and renewed.

I would like you now to all think about one of your deepest desires.

When you have something in mind face north and visualise a Lord of the Forest. Go to him and whisper your desire to him. He will offer you a pine cone to represent your wish embodied. Thank him and pay your respects to the Earth.

Now turn to face the east and visualise a Lady of the Sands. Go to her. She greets you and bids you to plant your desire (i.e. the pine cone) deep in the sand where it will be safe and nurtured. Thank her and pay your respects to the Wind and the Sun.

Now turn to the west and visualise the Ocean Mother. Go to her. She bids you to cleanse your hands in the water of life. After this, she blesses you and offers you a token of your journey... Thank her and pay your respects to the Water.

The Priestess joins the circle and holds hands with the people next to her and indicates everyone else to join hands too. As the circle starts to turn, everyone walks deosil to raise energy.

When the energy has been raised, the High Priestess throws her arms up to the skies, releasing the power to fulfil the desires of all present and the remainder for the Universe to use where it sees fit.

She moves away from the circle, to close it. First she moves to the north, raising her arms to the skies and saying:

Element of earth, thank you for lending your strength and stability this night.
Hail and farewell!

She moves to the west, raising her arms to the skies and saying:

Element of water, thank you for blessing us with loving emotions so right.
Hail and farewell!

She moves to the south, raising her arms to the skies and saying:

Element of fire, many thanks for your passion and illuminating light.
Hail and farewell.

She moves to the east, raising her arms to the skies and saying:

Element of air, we appreciate your winds of change that swirl within our lives.
Hail and farewell.

Returning to the centre, holding her arms wide and slowly bringing them in to cross her chest as she speaks to thank the God, she says:

Herne the Hunter, thank you for showing us the magic of nature and for teaching us the lessons of the wise. We thank you for your energies today and bid you hail and farewell!

Holding her arms wide and slowly bringing them in to cross her chest as she speaks to thank the Goddess, she says:

By all the powers of autumn and Elen's sacred springs, energy and transformation, Elen of the Ways we thank you for your energies today and bid you hail and farewell!

Standing in the centre, bringing her hands together, she says:

As the circle dissipates and the energies depart we leave here with love and peace in our hearts.
This circle is open and never broken for we are friends, brothers and sisters. Merry we meet and merry we part to meet merry again another day. Blessed be!

She passes round slices of warm apple pie and cinnamon cookies.

Samhain Ritual by Joshua Petchey

Cover the altar in a white cloth if you can to represent the eternal spirit. The earth is moving into the darkness of winter, but it is an eternal cycle. The white represents how the earth and all of us live, die and are reborn once more. Or, if you prefer, decorate it in black for the winter to come or orange for the fading autumn.

Ensure you have some marigolds present as they represent the powers of clairvoyance and psychic abilities and are used around Samhain in many cultures for this reason. If you know it, also have a deceased loved one's favourite flower present or maybe even one that reminds you of them. This will help with the intent to bring them forward. Place some crystals of your own choosing on the altar too, maybe a mixture of crystals such as amethyst for a higher plane and the crown chakra with some jasper or onyx for our physical plane and the root chakra. This can represent the merging of two realms. If you have a picture of the spirit, this would also be good to place on the altar – maybe next to some incense; sandalwood for clairvoyance or rose for love if appropriate.

As well as all this, try to decorate the altar with some food. If you are skilled with a spatula and oven, then you can bake or cook all sorts of Samhain-type dishes, whether it be cinnamon cakes, beef pies or pumpkin bread. But if not, then just basic fresh foods will do such as pumpkins, squash, pomegranates, etc. Make sure to have some apples present as they will come in handy later on.

Also include a pretty candle on the altar. You can colour it as you wish, choose whichever colour feels relevant to you. Light it when you begin, but also ensure you have a cauldron or something fireproof too.

Casting the circle

Many gathered in this place.
A wealth of energy to protect.
A union of friendship, love and grace.
A home for realms to intersect.
Mother Earth and Father Sky, come to us in this domain.
Cast this circle of transcendent light.
Purge this space of curse and bane.

Within this sphere of divine protection.
Our energies spiral, grow and soar.
To learn of love and our souls' perfection.
To honour those who have come before.

Quarter calls

Guardians of the west, spirit of water, we summon thee.
In this time of reflection we look to you the most.
You are the element of love and of emotion.
Like water we can reflect on the memories of what has come
before, in this year or in this life.
You bring the flow of emotion, the balance of light and dark,
joy and sorrow; but only through this balance can we find our
harmony.
So have us feel that which our hearts neglect and remember
that which our minds reject.
Hail and welcome!

Guardians of the north, spirit of earth, we summon thee.
As the dark winter approaches we look to you for guidance.
You teach us all the beauty in stillness, the wisdom in silence.
As the New Year begins, a time of uncertainty, help us to
remain strong so we can look within ourselves.
Going deep to find the seed of potential that lies within all
existence, we can nurture that seed to bring our own new
growth for the coming year.
Hail and welcome!

Guardians of the east, spirit of air, we summon thee.
The veil between worlds has dropped, realities shift between
one another.
The opportunity has come to connect to those who we have
lost.
The element of air can bring clarity to our minds and intuition

to our hearts so we may see the truth within ourselves, break through the fog of uncertainty that blinds us from other realms and find the inspiration to bring light into our future. Hail and welcome!

Guardians of the south, spirit of fire, we summon thee.
The year has ended we head into darkness.
And within this darkness we must begin to slow and find peaceful stillness.
But within us all burns our infinite fire ready to consume us and transform us.
We ask of you to cleanse our souls and purify our bodies to find growth through this transition.
Bring us the courage to burn in these flames so we may be reborn from the ashes.
Hail and welcome!

Deity invocations

God of the underworld, Hades, we invoke thee.
Guide of the spirits, lord of the dead, we ask of thee to open the gates of the underworld.
Release our ancestors for this day, ushering them to this realm so we may once again commune with those who have come before us.
Hail and welcome!

Goddess of the underworld, Persephone, we invoke thee.
Queen of the dead, Goddess of the spring, you make your descent into the underworld at this time. You have aided many souls to pass from this life and back again.
Bring us our ancestors steal them from the clutches of darkness, returning them to us.
Hail and welcome!

Ancestor invocation

I summon spirits of those once lost, ancestors, loved ones, family and friends.

Doorways opened to be crossed from somatic realms we shall ascend.

We welcome thee unto this place.

This circle of trust, truth and amity.

Ideas of reality to be erased.

Enlighten our minds with transcendent clarity.

Those taking part in the ritual now spend time in ancestral remembrance. The person leading the ritual says:

Take this time to have some peace and quiet. Sit on the ground connect with the earth and the universe. Just go within, have the time to remember those who have come before, relatives, loved ones, etc. Really try to connect with them, see them in your mind's eye. Those spirits will be around you this time of year more than any other. Talk to them, give them messages. See what happens next. What feelings do you get? Making note of all your senses, any visions, sounds, tastes or smells. Anything, no matter how insignificant, could be the message from the spirit. Any feeling at all, if it resonates with you, then listen to it.

The Mystery of the Apple

The person leading the ritual says:

The apple is the universal symbol of wisdom. It has been used at this time of year for centuries. And, as we know, has evolved into such Samhain games as apple bobbing. Although in the past there were all sorts of apple games, including ones with fire, I wouldn't recommend trying these more dangerous ones now.

The apple is said to house great knowledge and immortality within it. It was once said that to peel an apple gave you the ability to foretell how long you would live. The longer the peel is unbroken, the longer you will live. It is also said that within the realm of the dead stands an apple tree that bears fruit indefinitely. And to eat the fruit ourselves gives us psychic ability to commune with the deceased. Hence how apples became so popular at Samhain.

So for the next task take an apple and pass it around or each person take an apple for their own. Cut the apple widthways through the middle to reveal the pentagram within. This pentagram represents all of nature, physical, metaphysical and divine. And with this apple take the time to sit quietly with nature once more. But this time have a think about the time of year it is. After all, Samhain marks the end of summer and autumn and the beginning of winter and the darkness to come. Have a think about nature at this time; the colours, the smells, the fruits and so forth. Once again look within. But this time assess your own body and how it feels. Think about how the buzz of energetic summer has waned and the relaxing stillness of winter approaches. Try to connect with the earth to instil within your body the message of winter nature has to offer.

Endings

Samhain is known as the witches' New Year. It is the end of the lively summer and the beginning of the tranquil (if not quite chilly) winter. As an ending it is important that we recognise the changes in our lives and utilise this upcoming start of the year as a time to let go of the past year. Take all that serves you and all that brings you happiness into this New Year and remove that which does not.

On a piece of paper have everyone write something or a list of somethings that they wish to let go of. This can be anything they choose, whether it is people, places, habits or thoughts. Once this is done have them cross out what they have written, visualising the cross as their intent to banish. Then, most importantly, write under this crossed-out list a new list of things they wish to bring into their lives; positivity coming in to replace the negativity going out. Then, when all is written, have everyone use the altar candle to light their piece of paper, dropping it into a cauldron or fireproof dish. Say:

As it burns, visualise the intent of this exchange of positivity and negativity flowing to the universe to come to fruition.

Dumb supper

There is as act known as a dumb supper. This is something done by people at this time of year where an extra place setting will be made out for the spirit of a loved one who is invoked. Then everyone stays silent (hence the 'dumb' part) and eats the meal, thinking of their loved one. So as departed loved ones have already been called into circle, if you want and if you have any food on the altar you wish to consume, take some and enjoy the food. Eat an apple, drink some pomegranate juice (chew on a piece of squash if you wish to), but also leave some food and drink for the spirits within the circle. As you eat and drink, think about them once more feeling as though you are sharing the meal with them.

Ancestor farewell

Spirits of loved ones, all who are present.
We have connected, conversed and shared.
You have aided our hopes, wishes and intent.
We have looked within, our souls are bared.
From within this circle you may withdraw,
but stay forever in our hearts and minds.

As the beloved memory of what came before,
And as the hallowed spirit, both entwined.

Deity Farewells

Goddess Persephone, Queen of the Underworld.
We thank you for your aid in this rite.
Before your descent into the underworld.
You have delivered us those whom we hold most dear.
Take care of them in their returning journey.
Hail and farewell!

Hades, God of the Underworld, Lord of the Dead.
We thank you for your aid in this rite.
You have allowed us to connect with our loved ones.
Giving us the gift only you can bestow upon us.
May you stay forever the guide to those whom we have lost.
Hail and farewell!

Quarter closings

Guardians of the south, spirit of fire, we thank you.
You have helped us to purify our souls to look within and start anew in this time of transformation. We shall keep our inner embers glowing bright through this cold winter so we may begin to burn again, reborn once more this coming spring.
Hail and farewell!

Guardians of the east, spirit of air, we thank you.
You have taught us to see clearly in this universe.
We have connected with our ancestors as you have gifted us the clarity to view the world beyond this realm of physicality.
Hail and farewell!

Guardians of the north, spirit of earth, we thank you.

You have guided us on our journey inwards to find our own potential.

Through silence and stillness we have connected with the earth and discovered its beauty.

May we greet this coming darkness with patience and tranquillity.

Hail and farewell!

Guardians of the west, spirit of water, we thank you.

You have aided us in our reflections of ourselves.

To look back on this past year remove all that which does not serve and find the harmonious healing we so desire.

May we now look to a future of happiness and love.

Hail and farewell!

Circle uncasting

We have gathered in this place.

This blessed ground is our retreat.

We have learnt of love in all its forms.

Now the ritual is complete.

Mother Earth and Father Sky our words have now been spoken.

May this circle now dissipate, uncast, but never broken.

So mote it be!

Esbat Rituals

So what is an esbat? It sounds like a model of car; 'Oh, I drove here in my Ford Esbat...'

Esbats are working celebrations usually held on particular Moon phases so they are essentially lunar parties. Magic can be worked on each different phase of the Moon to add extra oomph and rituals can be held around those magical workings. I have given an introduction to working Moon magic together with Moon phase rituals in my book *Pagan Portals: Moon Magic,* but here is a very basic guide:

Waxing Moon : Good for healing rituals, positive magic, luck, prosperity, new plans or projects and generally growth of any kind.

Full Moon: Good for your psychic abilities, energy, working with the lunar Goddesses, fertility rituals, changes, strength, power and transformations. I like to also use the Full Moon for divination and for charging and cleansing crystals and magical tools.

Waning Moon: Good for removing curses and hexes, ending relationships, reversing spells and undoing negative influences. It is a time to let go and release all that no longer serves you.

Celtic Tree Rituals

Our coven also held rituals one year that all corresponded to the Celtic tree calendar, each ritual was a different tree and we worked magic that aligned with the magical properties.

Holly Moon Ritual Including Dragons by Rachel Patterson and Tracey Roberts

Casting the circle

Drum as the circle is walked deosil, then say:

We cast a circle of light
Strong with all a dragon's might
A safe and strong protective shield
Coloured dragons of all the shades
This circle is bound with dragon strength
This circle is cast, so mote it be!

Quarter calls

Mighty Dragon, guardian of the realms of the east.
With graceful spirit, swift of flight and bringing the purity of truth.
Hail and welcome!

Mighty Dragon, guardian of the realms of the south.
With flames of inspiration and passion and bringing strength.
Hail and welcome!

Mighty Dragon, guardian of the realms of the west.
With waves of emotional and spiritual energy and cleansing our souls.

Hail and welcome!
Mighty Dragon, guardian of the realms of the north.
With wisdom, strength and knowledge and bringing stability
and growth.
Hail and welcome!

Deity calls

Hail Morgana, Queen of the Fey, tamer of Dragons.
You who ride the winds of night and weave the magic of
crystal and sword, we call you.
Join us in our rite today, strengthen our magic and teach us
the hidden secrets of nature that wait just below the surface.
Weaver, cunning woman, you whose voice calls the Dragon,
be with us and lead us safely.
Hail and welcome!

Merlin, Old One, Grandfather Druid, hear us across the mists
of time.
We sing your praises, spar with our rhymes, ancient bard,
magic maker, come into our midst this day.
We seek your wisdom, your inner sight. Merlin, magician,
Dragon tamer, this day will you be our guide.
Come forth from the cavern where you hide.
Hail and welcome!

We call upon the dryad of the holly tree
Whose leaves are like spear points in the forest
And whose berries are like drops of drawn blood
Bring with you the strength and protection of the warrior
Teaching us to be courageous in all that we do
Holly tree, spirit of earth.
We bid you hail and welcome!

Reading

So holly...a winter tree surely? Well, yes, when you think of holly it probably brings to mind red berries and the winter solstice, but the Celts named their eighth month from July 8th to August 5th after the holly. Although we are still in the height of summer, the Holly Month brings with it the start of the waning year. The Oak King has been defeated and now is the time of the Holly King's reign. As the days grow shorter, the energy of the Sun is transferred into the Earth, highlighting our practical needs and desires.

The holly is long associated with warrior energy and in the past spear shafts were made from its wood as were clubs wielded by the wild Celts and warrior Gods. The leaves of this tree begin life soft and pliable, but like the warrior, they soon harden to form an impenetrable barrier and the berries are associated with fire and sacrifice.

The Celtic fire festival of Lughnasadh begins the harvest on August 1st and as such the month of the holly is a time to give thanks for your blessings, so we will take a few moments now to give thanks for what we have and to appreciate the good things in your life. If anyone would like to share what they are thankful for then please feel free.

Raising energy

All join in with drumming and walking the circle to raise a cone of energy, which the High Priestess releases to the universe for healing when ready.

This is followed by a feast of cake and mead.

Dragon lore

The High Priestess says:

Dragons are a primeval force, they are physical and spiritual, they bring with them the full force and power of the elements.

They are also very wise and intelligent.

Dragon energy is one of the most powerful energies I know of and when blended together via the four main elements, creates the Etheric Dragon...a super power.

Dragon energy is linear, so be careful what you ask for. You will receive it in the most direct way possible. Be very specific about your intentions, integrity and intelligence. Dragons do not necessarily use human logic, if you offer them a problem they will find a solution, but it will be a straight-forward one, removing anything in its path to solve it...

Dragon energy is very good at removing dark energy. It is good for clearing negative energy, but make sure you also ask for positive energy to be left in its place. And I have found it is always best to end your request with 'and do no harm'. Dragon magic works quickly and can sometimes have unexpected results.

Dragons also have so much to teach us, all that ancient wisdom waiting to be shared with us not to mention all their powerful energy and support that they can provide us with.

Closing

Dryad of the holly tree, spirit of the earth.
We thank you for joining us today and bringing us your warrior energies to aid our rite.
We bid you, hail and farewell!

Merlin, to our circle you have come, teaching us your ancient ways, of magic, wisdom, lines that ley. Merlin, wise one, return to the past, we honour and respect your lessons and ask you leave us with your blessing.
Hail and farewell!

Morgana, as we depart for our daily lives and as you depart for your shadowed realm, we thank you for the secrets you

have shown to us, for the workings you have strengthened.
We bid you farewell for now, lady of magic and enchantment,
until we meet again.
Hail and farewell!

Releasing the quarters

Mighty Dragon, guardian of the realms of the north.
We thank you for your aid in our rite and we bid you
Hail and farewell!

Mighty Dragon, guardian of the realms of the west.
We thank you for your aid in our rite and we bid you
Hail and farewell!

Mighty Dragon, guardian of the realms of the south.
We thank you for your aid in our rite and we bid you
Hail and farewell!

Mighty Dragon, guardian of the realms of the east.
We thank you for your aid in our rite and we bid you
Hail and farewell!

Uncasting the circle

All walk the circle widdershins. The High Priestess says:
We uncast the circle of light
That was created with the dragon's might
A safe and strong protective shield
The energy released
This circle is unwound
So mote it be!

Alder Moon Ritual by Rachel Patterson and Tracey Roberts

Casting the circle

The High Priestess walks the circle deosil, scattering herbs. She says:

Casting this circle with white, energy woven from the maiden's light
Casting this circle red, energy woven from the mother instead
Casting this circle black, crone energy woven that we lack
This circle is cast may it protect those within and that without

Calling the quarters

The High Priestess stands in the centre holding four pieces of coloured ribbon, handing one end to each quarter caller. As they call, the HPs holds onto the other end.

Mountains, valleys, fields and desserts, the spirit of rocks, stones and fertile soil.
Mother Nature stirs beneath the earth, as she sends up new shoots and the fresh beginnings of life from her belly. Now the day and night are in perfect balance, we stand within the portal of dark and light. We ask the element of earth to join us today, bring with you stability and grounding.
Hail and welcome!

Strong winds, floating clouds, a gentle breeze.
As the winds of change bring with them warmer weather, cleansing and refreshing us.
Now we cast behind us the bleakness of winter and the past and look forward to that which lies before us. We ask the element of air to join us today, bring with you intellect and new ideas.

Hail and welcome!

Flames of the fire and the candle, volcanoes and bonfires. Father Sun begins to bring more warmth and light, helping the new life grow. Now is the time of planting seeds in the physical, mental and spiritual planes. May our desires and dreams be made manifest. We ask the element of fire to join us today, bringing passion and energy.
Hail and welcome!

Drops of spring rain, splashing puddles, waterfalls and rivers. The water joins with the other elements to help the plant life on its way. May the very waters that bring life to this land carry our thoughts and aspirations with them, with the confidence that our feelings are safe and will return to us as potential if our requests are honourable.
We ask the element of water to join us today, bringing positive emotions.
Hail and welcome!

The High Priestess stands in the centre and says:

As I bring together the four elements of earth, air, fire and water, they join with the fifth element of spirit, binding together as one.

The High Priestess ties the four coloured ribbons in a loose knot together as she speaks, and lays it on the altar, as the quarter callers let their ends of the ribbon drop.

Calling deity

The High Priestess says:

I call to the Goddess of Fertility, Freya, who has awakened

from her winter slumber.

Her magic sweeps across the land bringing new life, we honour her and bring harmony into our lives with the coming of the new season.

As the sap rises in all living things, the old is replaced by the new.

We bid you hail and welcome!

I call to the God of Light, Innocence and Fertility, Baldur. Share with us the power of your strength.

Let us see and feel your presence in the midst of our circle and the energy that you bring effect us all as we open our circle to you.

We bid you hail and welcome!

I call upon the Dryad of the Alder to bring balance and inspired action to our ritual today.

Bring with you perspective, protection, firm foundations and new challenges.

Bring the balance between the inner and outer worlds.

We bid you hail and welcome!

The High Priestess smudges those present, then says:

We have chosen to call upon Norse deities today, Freya and Baldur.

In Norse mythology, Freya is a Goddess of love and fertility, and the most beautiful and propitious of the Goddesses. She is the patron Goddess of crops and birth, the symbol of sensuality and was called upon in matters of love. She loves music, spring and flowers, and is particularly fond of the elves. Freya is one of the foremost Goddesses of the Vanir.

Baldur is a God of light, joy, purity, beauty, innocence, and reconciliation. Son of Odin and Frigg, he was loved by both Gods and men and was considered to be the best of the Gods. He had a good character, was friendly, wise and eloquent.

We are here to celebrate the Alder Moon.

The alder represents a balanced perspective, preservation, protection, challenge, discrimination and firm foundations.

Traditional the alder was the haunt of faeries and was associated with protecting the faerie realms. Water spirits or undines are said to protect this tree and it is also linked with unicorns.

It is a tree of balance, associated with both water and fire. It has a dynamic fiery energy, while its roots are deep in water providing intuition and inspiration from within.

The buds of the alder are set in spirals, which are a powerful symbol of everlasting life and resurrection.

Alder brings balance between the inner and the outer worlds, between our intuitive receptive selves and our rational logical selves. It helps us to harness discrimination as we find our way through life's challenges. Alder helps us to see beyond the obvious and to work with the knowledge of the past and to follow our instincts.

Use the potential and fertility of this time to create opportunities for positive change in our lives and in the world.

Ribbon tree

The ribbon tree is represented by a small branch fixed into a pot of earth. The High Priestess passes around a bowl full of ribbon strips. She says:

We have a ribbon tree here, if you would like to, take a piece of ribbon from the basket being passed around, any colour. Go with your instinct and pick the first one you see. Then hold the ribbon in your hand and think about a new venture, a promise, a new beginning for yourself – something you would like to start working on or with. Send that thought energy into the ribbon. When you are ready step forward and tie the ribbon onto the tree.

I will keep the tree with all the ribbons on until Beltane and then we will burn the ribbons to release the energy as they will have worked their magic by then.

When everyone has done that, the HPs says:

If everyone would like to hold hands we will raise some energy to send to those that are in need and to the planet in general.

This is followed by feasting and then closing words.

Closing

We thank the Dryad of the Alder trees for joining us today and bringing with you the spirit of balance and potential.
We bid you hail and farewell.

Bringer of joy and fruitfulness, we thank you for being with us this day.
May our lives always reflect the gifts you give us and may we be ever mindful of your role in the turning of the seasons.
We bid you hail and farewell.

We thank the Goddess for her presence, warmth and gentleness in bringing each season at its given time.
May we show that appreciation in our love of nature and its many faces over the turning wheel of the year.
We honour the Goddess at this time of renewal.
We bid you hail and farewell.

Releasing the quarters

The High Priestess picks up the tied ribbons and gives one end to each of the quarter callers.

Blessings to the element of water, the place of rest and renewal.

To the seas and oceans that are vital for our very existence and the varied creatures that reside therein.

May your fluidity of thought stay with us reminding us of our part within nature and the responsibility we have.

We thank you for being here with us today.

We bid you hail and farewell.

Blessings to the element of fire and the vision of long warm days and nights filled with the sounds and smells of nature that are on their way.

To the return of our feathered friends who winter in faraway places and to the creatures that awake at the call of the rising temperatures.

We thank you for being here with us today.

We bid you hail and farewell.

Blessings to the element of air for lifting our spirits at this ritual today.

To the rising of the life-giving Sun and the joy that we all feel as each passing day lengthens.

May our days be warm and our skies be blue as we come out of winter into the budding season.

We thank you for being here with us today.

We bid you hail and farewell.

Blessings to the element of earth for inspiring us with your presence.

To the vast open spaces that leave us in awe and wonderment, and the many creatures that inhabit those spaces, we thank

you for being here with us today.
We bid you hail and farewell.

Blessings to the element of spirit for your presence.
In the love of the God and Goddess we gathered together to celebrate today.
May the God and Goddess take the collective energy from this circle and give it to the trees by which we stand as a token of our love and appreciation for the privilege of being here.
Blessed be.

The High Priestess unties the ribbons. She walks the circle widdershins and says:

Maiden uncast your circle white, release your web of glowing light
Mother uncast your circle red, release the strands of glowing threads
Old Crone, uncast your circle black, we thank you for the knowledge that we lacked
By the elements of earth, air, fire and water
This circle is open but never broken
So mote it be!

Other Ritual Examples

Rituals can be held for any reason and any occasions. Here I am very pleased to be able to share some Kitchen Witch Coven rituals that have been co-written by coven members that we held as open rituals in a local forest along with others that have been shared with me by very lovely people.

Kitchen Witch Ritual: Earth – Co-Written by Rachel Patterson, Tracey Roberts, Vanessa Armstrong, Joshua Petchey, Sue Perryman and Samantha Leaver

Rachel speaks as the circle is walked:

> Casting this circle with white, energy woven from the maiden's light
> Casting this circle red, energy woven from the mother instead
> Casting this circle black, crone energy woven that we lack
> This circle is cast may it protect those within and that without

A staff is passed around to each person in the circle asking them to state out loud one word that they associate with earth such as soil, mountains, rocks, stability and grounding.

Tracey:

> I call to the Dark God, Horned God of the Forest Come as Herne, the Green Man, Cernunnos, Pan. Come as protector of the land and guardian of the gateways.
> Teach us the mysteries of the standing stone, blood and bone.

Help us to be as silent and receptive as the deepest, darkest cave.

As we listen for the soft echo of the voices of our ancestors Horned One, we invite you into our circle.

Hail and welcome!

Josh:

God of the Mountains, Atlas, I call on thee.

You are the God of strength, the master of endurance.

The Titan sentenced to hold up the sky and the stars.

You spend eternity living with the weight of the universe on your shoulders.

In this time; the cold, still, silence of winter, bestow upon us your gift of durability.

So we may learn to tackle the obstacles of our lives and make it through this time of darkness with quiet strength.

Hail and welcome!

Sue:

I call upon Gaia, Mother Earth, our home and our foundation.

All life springs from your fertile womb and to you one day all life will return.

First born of Chaos you sustain all life with your fruits from the rich soil and bring nurturing, healing, balance and harmony to our lives.

Great Mother, creator of Gods and humanity who brought forth the Earth, the heavens and the seas. Teach us to love, respect and honour all your creations and to tread lightly upon the earth.

Hail and welcome!

Ness:

I call upon Ceres, Goddess of the Grain and Fertile Earth you have the power to feed our lands you give us the gift of harvest.

Teach us how to sow our seeds of life, to nurture
ourselves and to grow strong.
So that we may reap a bountiful harvest.
Hail and welcome!

The circle is smudged, then the deities are introduced.

Tracey:

The Horned God can be a much misunderstood deity.
He is an archetype for the male elemental force of
nature, but the Christian Church, being unable to tame
his wild spirit, named him the Devil. They instilled fear
for something they didn't understand and couldn't
control. To people walking a pagan pathway the Horned
God represents the wildness of the natural world. He is
the Lord of the Forest, vegetation and all animals. He is
also the Guardian of the Underworld and Lord of Death.
But to me the Horned God is also about balance and the
natural order of things. He is the divine masculine that
balances the fierce femininity of the Goddess. He is the
Sun to her Moon. He is the deep darkness of night and
the darkest depths of the forest, but also the bringer of
light and blazing fiery Sun. He is the Lord of the Hunt
but also the hunted. He is guardian of the gateway to the
underworld, bringer of death, but also the God of rebirth
and life. There are many horned or antlered Gods from
different cultures. As the God of vegetation, he is
Dionysus, the Green Man, Adonis and Damuzi. He is the
shamanic God of the wildwood Cernunnos. As Lord of
the Hunt he is Herne the Hunter. As God of the flock he
is known as Pan. And as Lord of the Underworld he is
Osiris or Apis. And there are so many other examples.
I've walked with him in all his forms since my pagan
path began and for me it's all about the antlers!

Josh:

Atlas is generally seen as a Titan. Even though in my research he is sometimes considered a God and sometimes a primordial deity (meaning he was here at the beginning like Gaia and Uranus). But I generally like to think of him as a Titan. So as the story goes he was grandson of Gaia and Uranus. When the whole 'Gods of Olympus rising up against Cronus and castrating him' thing happened, the Titans were all punished in one form or another. Atlas' punishment was, of course, to hold up the sky and the stars. Often any statue of Atlas will be of him with the celestial sphere being carried on his shoulders. Atlas, as you can imagine, became known as the Titan of mountains and endurance. His name literally means those two words. And congratulations to him – he got a mountain range and an ocean named after him. Now the story of Atlas continues in two different ways from what I can gather. The first is that Perseus, son of Poseidon, decapitated Medusa and used the petrifying abilities of her severed head to turn Atlas to stone. It is said that this was to spare him of the weight of the sky as if he were stone it wouldn't require any effort to keep holding it. Although in my opinion, I'd still feel bad for Atlas because now he can't even scratch his nose.

Anyway, the second of the stories I read has to do with Hercules. All told different, but I'll go with this one. It is said that Hercules wished to get a golden apple from the garden of Hera. But these apples were guarded by the Hesperides, daughters of Atlas. So Hercules waltzed on over to mountainous Atlas and asked him to retrieve a golden apple from his daughters and in return he would hold the sky for him temporarily. Atlas agreed, went to his daughters and managed to bring back the golden apple Hercules had asked for. Feeling incredibly grateful that Atlas had got the apple and then returned to his post, Hercules decided to give him a gift. He used his God-like strength to move a couple of mountains around (as you do) and created 'The Pillars of Hercules', two large mountains either side of the world to hold up the sky. So thankfully poor Atlas got to be relieved of his turmoil. Where he went from this point on I have no idea, but I hope it's somewhere nice.

Sue:

Gaia was the first Greek deity who emerged from Chaos. She is Mother Earth who created our planet, the universe, the first Gods and humanity. She gave birth to Uranus, the sky and Pontus the sea and then she mated with Uranus and gave birth to the twelve Titans, the Cyclops and three monsters. Uranus was horrified by his offspring and shut them into the depths of the earth. This angered Gaia who persuaded one of the Titans, Cronus, to castrate Uranus as he slept beside her. The blood dropping on the land gave birth to the Erinyes, Goddesses of vengeance and justice, to giants and to the ash tree nymphs the Meliae; and the blood dropping on the sea produced Aphrodite.

Gaia is a primal Mother Goddess. She was believed to be a prophetess, the oracle at Delphi is said to have belonged to her before it passed to Apollo. She presided over marriages and was offered the first fruits and grains from every harvest, black sheep were sacrificed to her. The Greeks believed that an oath sworn on Gaia was the strongest of all since no-one could escape from the Earth herself. Gaia is often seen as the personification of the Earth and sometimes as a beautiful woman half buried in earth. She is Mother Nature who is always working to maintain harmony, healing, wholeness and balance within the environment.

Ness:

Ceres is an Earth deity, being a Goddess of the grain and of the harvest. Taking care of the lands, the crops and the flowers was what she did best. She was loved by mankind as she watched and nurtured the crops. Ceres was also a doting mother to her daughter Proserpina. When Proserpina was snatched from her home to live with Pluto in the Underworld, Ceres pined for her daughter so much so that the crops and flowers pined with her and withered and died. Ceres wandered the caverns of the Underworld trying to find her daughter, lighting the way with candles. Only when Proserpina was allowed to live with her mother for the six months of the year were the crops allowed to grow and flourish. Ceres is also said to be Goddess of Transition, protecting women at various transitions of their lives from childhood to womanhood and the time of change between unmarried, married and motherhood. She is often depicted with a harvesting tool in one hand and carrying a basket of grain or fruit in the other wearing a garland of wheat ears on her head.

Rachel:

Earth is the element of stability, foundations and of the body. The Earth is the realm of wisdom, knowledge, strength, growth and prosperity. It is also the physical Earth on which we live and the very heart of life. It is essential in spells and rituals of prosperity, business, fertility and stability. Earth is a feminine element and governs stone and knot magic.

The Earth can be viewed as our mother, with its fertile and nurturing farmland, providing all the planet's creatures with nourishment and shelter. In its physical manifestations, such as stones, rocks, crystals and gems, the element of earth represents the densest of the elements.

The Earth is the womb from which all things spring. Pressing your hand against fresh soil, you can feel its vitality, stability and earthiness. In its fertile soil, we've grown the food that provides life, on its surface we live out our lives.

This earth energy not only exists within ourselves, but also throughout the universe at large.

Herb pouches

The HPS hands out brown fabric pouches for everyone to fill with each earth-related item having charged them before popping into the pouches. Descriptions of the magical properties, myths and history of each herb/spice are read out. Information can be taken from my books *A Kitchen Witch's World of Magical Herbs & Plants* and *A Kitchen Witch's World of Magical Food.*

Mugwort

Mugwort Magical Properties: Strength, psychic powers, protection, dreams, healing, astral travel, feminine energy, cleansing

Salt

Salt Magical Properties: Cleansing, purification, protection

Sesame

Sesame Magical Properties: Prosperity, protection, energy, strength, secrets

Oats

Oats Magical Properties: Passion, fertility, prosperity

Twigs and pebbles
Send everyone into the forest to find a small twig and pebble each.

Pasta
Pasta Magical Properties: Psychic powers, protection, communication, creativity

Gaia Serpent Meditation

Sam:

Begin now by closing your eyes.

Make yourself comfortable, ground and centre in your usual way.

Take a slow deep breath in, holding for a moment and exhale gently.

With each breath that you take, simply allow your mind to relax.

Just allow the worries of your day to fade away.

If you experience any unwanted thoughts simply repeat the words 'silence now'.

Breathe in, holding the breath for a moment and then exhale gently.

We are going on a journey now to experience the spirit of Mother Earth – Gaia.

The spirit of Gaia knows who you are and wishes to help you on your journey.

The spirit of Gaia is alive, dressed in her autumn robes she wishes to guide and assist us in crossing the veil.

All you have to do is be still and tune into the vibration of the planet.

You are outside in a field at the beginning of a path. You smell autumn rains on cool earth, you watch as the last golden leaves fall from very nearly bare branches

The air is crisp with a chilly breeze; the Sun hangs low in the sky brushing gentle evening rays across your skin as it is chased across the sky by peaches and pinks.

You walk up a slight incline, through a tunnel of vines still heavy with fat red grapes. Along the way you notice bowls of honey and barley. You pick up a bowl to make an offering to the spirits you are sure to meet today.

You reach a plateau and realise you are high in a mountain range; the air is thin where the Earth reaches high up into the skies. At this plateau you are faced with an ancient stone circle, around the circumference are burning torches. A mist of deep earthy patchouli smoke rises from the centre. You approach. In the middle is a spring rising at great speed from the centre of the Earth, a crystal clear and hot pool has formed.

In the middle of the pool is a stone island. A fierce looking serpent sits staring out at his visitor with brown and green scales and piercing yellow eyes.

'I guard this sacred space, ancient Delphi, for Mother Gaia, you seek guidance from the womb of the Earth?' He hisses through your mind.

Listen carefully to the serpent's message.

Before you leave this place remember to thank the spirit of Gaia by throwing the honey and barley mixture into the spring. Move slowly, leave this place and trace your steps back down the incline through the tunnel of fat red grapes.

Find yourself returning to the small field where your journey began.

Breathe in, holding the breath for a moment and then exhale gently, feel your mind coming back to the present.

Breathe in again, holding your breath for a moment

and exhale gently, feel your toes and fingers and wiggle them.

And open your eyes.

Those present share cakes and drink.

Closing thanks to the Earth

Ness:

Ceres, thank you for your presence in this circle today.

For showing us how to connect with the Earth that we stand on.

And in turn connecting with ourselves and each other to grow and to share our harvests.

Hail and farewell!

Sue:

Gaia, thank you for sharing in our ritual today, for reminding us that all life is sacred and teaching us love, compassion and understanding for all your creatures.

May we become guardians of the Earth and teach future generations to respect honour and nurture all of nature and all of life.

Hail and farewell!

Josh:

Colossal Titan, Atlas. You were rewarded for your service to this realm.

You learnt the earthly lesson of patience and endurance. Finding harmony in your freedom from your time of stillness.

We too have learnt of power today.

You have taught us the meaning of having strength in silence.

And from this newfound wisdom, we thank you.

Hail and farewell!

Tracey:

We thank the Dark God, Horned One of the Forest Herne, the Green Man, Cernunnos, Pan.

As we stand at the gateway to the dark half of the wheel.

We will listen in stillness as we begin our inward journeys.

Horned one, we thank you for your presence today.

Hail and farewell!

Uncasting the circle

Rachel:

Maiden uncast this circle white; unravel the threads of glowing light.

Mother uncast this circle red, unhook the tightly bound threads.

Crone uncast this circle black, allow us to keep the knowledge that we lacked.

This circle is open but never broken.

So mote it be.

Kitchen Witch Ritual: Air – Co-Written by Rachel Patterson, Tracey Roberts, Vanessa Armstrong and Joshua Petchey

Rachel says as the circle is walked:

Casting this circle with white, energy woven from the maiden's light

Casting this circle red, energy woven from the mother instead

Casting this circle black, crone energy woven that we lack

This circle is cast may it protect those within and that without

A staff is passed around to each person in the circle asking them to state out loud one word that they associate with air, such as wind, hurricane, clouds, intellect, intuition etc.

Tracey:

> I call on Athena, Greek Goddess of Wisdom.
> Bring clarity and freedom to our circle and our minds.
> Come Athena with your owl of gleaming eyes.
> Illuminate the hidden truths in our darkest recesses.
> Show us the way through change and let our spirits soar.
> Hail and welcome!

Josh:

> I call upon the Egyptian God of Air, Amun.
> You, the hidden one that breathes life into us all.
> Teach us to bring innovation into our thoughts at this time of year.
> As you the divine creator brought all into existence.
> May your feathers bring flight and freedom to our imagination.
> And through your mystery, may we see the unknown potential of our own minds.
> Hail and welcome!

Rachel:

> I call upon Ayao, Orisha of the Air, come forth from the forests and the eye of the tornadoes and bring your fierce strength to share your warrior skills with us today and allow us to learn from you and to be strong in our own hearts.
> Hail and welcome!

Ness:

> I call upon the God of the West Wind – Zephyrus.
> Greek winged youth of air – mild and gentle.
> As protector of plants, with your warm breath and humidity.

Nurturing our dreams and wishes, may we flourish in our inspiration.
As you bring the light spring and early summer breezes. Show us to be agile in thought and uninhibited in our possibilities.
Hail and welcome!

The circle is smudged.

Rachel:

With every breath we take we draw in a lungful of this wonderful element, without it we wouldn't last more than a few minutes.

The element of air rules intellect, thought, the first steps toward creation, movement, pure visualisation, spells involving travel, instruction, freedom, obtaining knowledge, discovering lost items and uncovering lies. It is the element of dreams and plans, goals and inventions. Air physically manifests as the sky, wind and the clouds.

In most witchcraft traditions, the element of air is located at the east of the ritual circle and is associated with dawn, the time of new beginnings. Incense is placed on the witch's altar to represent air and has long been used to carry prayers and appeals to the Gods by means of burning fragrance in the forms of incense or oils. Other items you might see on an altar would be feathers, wand or bells.

The element of air is vital to human survival, without it we would all perish, its aspects are thinness, motion and darkness and its quality is active. Air is the manifestation of movement, freshness, communication and of the intelligence. Sound is another manifestation of this element. As an element, it is invisible, but its reality can be felt in the air that we breathe in every day. To connect with the power of this element, find a place with clean air and breathe deeply, touch a feather or inhale the fragrance of a heavily scented flower. Let yourself experience the energy of this element, and reflect that we also possess air energy within ourselves. In magical terms, air is the power of the mind, the force of intellect, inspiration, imagination. It is ideas, knowledge, dreams and wishes. Air is the element of new life and new possibilities and is essential to spells and rituals of travel, instruction, finding lost items, some types of divination, and freedom. Air aids us in visualisation, a vital technique in magic. Air is a masculine element and governs the magic of the four winds. It is the vital spirit passing through all things, giving life to all things, moving and filling all things.

Herb pouches

All make herb pouches – yellow fabric bags are passed around and then each item to put inside it in turn, asking everyone to charge each item with their intent before adding it to the bag. Descriptions of the magical properties, myths and history of each herb/spice are read out. Information can be taken from my books *A Kitchen Witch's World of Magical Herbs & Plants* and *A Kitchen Witch's World of Magical Food*.

Feathers:
Feathers are used in spells and ceremonies to promote change. Every feather is a fetish (charm) and can become a sacred object.

Feathers are magically ruled by the element of air. This makes them good communication helpers. But each feather also can hold other special powers; depending on the bird it came from, its colour and place of discovery.

To charge a feather with your intent you need to hold the

feather in your hands in front of your mouth and slowly and gently breathe your intent into it. This charges the feather with your personal energy and magic.

Rice:

Rice Magical Properties: Prosperity, fertility, protection, rain, grounding, stability

Sage:

Sage Magical Properties: Protection, wishes, wisdom, purification, stimulating, intuition, abundance, success

Mint:

Mint Magical Properties: Money, healing, exorcism, protection, cleansing, calming

Parsley:

Parsley Magical Properties: Protection, purification, lust, happiness, fertility, spirit work

Star Anise:

Star Anise Magical Properties: Luck, psychic powers, purification, protection, dreams, spirituality, sleep

Cakes and drink

Everyone shares cakes and drink.

Closing and thanks to air

Ness:

Zephyrus – youthful God of Air, mild and gentle.
Thank you for your presence in this circle today.
Our dreams and wishes have been fulfilled and we have been inspired in our thoughts.

We bid you hail and farewell!

Rachel:

To Ayao, Orisha of the Air we thank you for your presence today and ask that you leave us with some of your strength, your warrior energy and positive thinking.

We bid you hail and farewell!

Josh:

Amun, Egyptian God of Air, We thank you for your aid in this rite.

You have brought innovation to our lives, freedom to our imaginations and helped to witness our own hidden potential.

We bid you hail and farewell!

Tracey:

Athena, we thank you for the clarity you brought to our circle today.

Our paths now illuminated and our journeys now clear, we bid you hail and Farewell

Rachel:

Maiden uncast this circle white; unravel the threads of glowing light.

Mother uncast this circle red, unhook the tightly bound threads.

Crone uncast this circle black, allow us to keep the knowledge that we lacked.

This circle is open but never broken.

So mote it be.

Kitchen Witch Ritual: Fire – Co-Written by Rachel Patterson, Tracey Roberts, Vanessa Armstrong and Joshua Petchey

Rachel speaks as the circle is walked:

Casting this circle with white, energy woven from the

maiden's light.

Casting this circle red, energy woven from the mother instead.

Casting this circle black, crone energy woven that we lack.

This circle is cast may it protect those within and that without.

A staff is passed around to each person in the circle asking them to state out loud a word that they associate with the element of fire, such as bonfire, volcano, passion, energy etc.

Tracey:

We call to you Wayland of the Spectral Smithy, Wayland of the forest forge, lord of smith craft and forger of the wyrd.

Teach us to find the beauty in broken things, even when it is us that are broken.

Give us the strength to overcome the wounds that may cripple us.

Help us to throw off our shackles and transform like a phoenix from the flames of your forge.

Inspire us to reach forever higher, soaring with an aim straight and true.

Wayland we invite you to our circle and ask for your blessings.

Hail and welcome!

Josh:

God of light, I invoke thee. Lucifer, King of Witches, keeper of magic.

Come to us, bringing with you your innate wisdom of spirituality.

You are the Archangel of enlightenment, and the God of glorious transformation.

Aid us to feed the flames within our souls, to evolve to the state of divinity you know we possess within ourselves.

You, the fallen betrayer, can help us to see your light, to sever the bonds of this earthly blindness, and purify our hearts.

Hail and welcome!

Rachel:

From Tahiti comes the woman Pele.

From the land of Bora-Bora.

From the rising mist of Kane, dawn swelling in the sky.

From the clouds blazing over Tahiti.

Restless yearning for Hawaii seized the woman Pele.

Built was the canoe, Honua-i-akea.

Your canoe, o Ka-moho-ali'I companion for voyaging.

Lashed securely and equipped was the canoe of the Gods.

The canoe for She Who Shapes the Sacred Land to sail in.

Pele, Goddess of Fire, we bid you hail and welcome!

Ness:

We call to you Hestia, Goddess of the Hearth and Home and Keeper of the Sacred Flame.

As Goddess of domestic life, bring with you happiness, warmth and blessings.

You are mild, gentle, forgiving, calm and well-centred.

May you inspire us to be these things in return.

Hail and welcome!

The circle is smudged.

Introduce the deities

Rachel:

In ancient Hawaii there were many Gods and

Goddesses; they were the spirits found in all things in the heavens and nature. One of these Goddesses, Hina, the supreme female spirit, gave birth to Pele. A few days after her birth Lonomakua, the keeper of the flame, saw the child and knew that she would become the keeper of the fire that burned deep in the Earth. She would hold the secrets of the fire and would one day rule the volcanoes of Hawaii. She would inherit the power to create and destroy land.

Pele appears in many forms from maiden to crone. She has the power to destroy, but what she actually does is reclaim land that has been desecrated by humankind, and she always provides us with the opportunity to keep balance. She is not destroying, she is reclaiming and restoring.

Madame Pele is the divine spark of creation and as such is an aspect of the divine mother. The word 'Aloha' hold the consciousness of the ancients placed there, 'Ah' is the first light of dawn, the spark of the divine, 'Lo' is the symbol and the sound of eternity, of forever. 'Ha' is breath, the gift, the blessing of life that comes from the divine. To say 'Aloha' is to remember our gift, what we have been given, it reminds us of our own inner greatness.

Josh:

Lucifer is the Roman God of Light. He is the brother of Diana and the counterpart of the Greek God of the Sun, Apollo, or sometimes Eos, God of the Dawn. His name 'Lucifer' means 'light bearer' as he is the star we see just before the dawn in the eastern sky. Later, in Christianity he became an archangel and brought with him the famous story of the angel turned away from heaven to become the evil betrayer, the Devil that so many have come to fear.

But the origin of this God goes back to when he was once known as 'King of Witches'. Lucifer and his light bearing ways teach us to see the light and the truth within us all. To look inwards to see the potential that each of us has, the potential for our spirits to evolve and ascend transforming to a state of divinity to become deity ourselves. And what we would call enlightenment other cultures thought to be a travesty, hence the reason he was given such a bad name.

So this God of light is associated with fire as he embodies all the spiritual, transformative and purifying energies of the element itself. He teaches us to have the confidence to let our inner light shine and the courage, if we must, to fall from grace.

Tracey:

Wayland is an Anglo Saxon God. He is a farrier, coin maker and all round creator of magnificent things for the Gods. Smiths have always been known for their potent magic and their ability to temper and transform metal into jewellery of incredible beauty and weapons of fearsome power. Wayland was once captured by a jealous king who wished to possess Wayland's services and have him work only for him. He kept Wayland a prisoner and in some stories has Wayland hamstrung so he can't escape. But Wayland bides his time and escapes anyway on wings he has fashioned himself. He said to reside in a burial mound on a hill in Berkshire and it is said that if you leave a coin and your horse there overnight, when you come back in the morning you will find your horse has been freshly shod. So Wayland not only blesses us with fiery transformation he also teaches us a little patience.

Ness:

Hestia is the Greek Goddess of the Hearth and Home.

Hestia was the first born of the Greek God Cronus and Goddess Rhea. Kronos heard that his children planned to overthrow him from his throne, so ate them. Hestia was the first to be swallowed and the last to be disgorged and is very often referred to as Hestia – the first and last. Hestia was at the centre of the family home – the hearth was the most important part of it. This was where families gathered and where food was prepared and eaten. She was also in charge of the Olympian hearths where she resided, and of the sacred flames. A Goddess associated with the element of fire, she was kind, gentle and welcoming – a bit like the warmth of our own fires on a cold, dark chilly evening. She has a vision that a house should be a home – a place where we replenish and are nurtured. A place of family, peace, security and comfort.

Rachel:

Fire is the element of change, strong will, energy and passion. It is most primal. It is the realm of sexuality and passion. It is not only the 'sacred fire' of sex, but also the spark of divinity, which shines within us and in all living things.

Fire rituals and spell work usually involve energy, authority, sex, healing, destruction (of negative habits or disease), purification, evolution and more.

Fire is masculine. It rules the south, the place of greatest heat, the colour red, and the season of summer.

Fire herb pouches

Everyone makes a pouch. Red fabric pouches are passed around the circle and then items that relate to fire, each one being charged with intent before popping the item into the pouch. Descriptions of the magical properties, myths and history of each herb/spice are read out. Information can be taken from my books

A Kitchen Witch's World of Magical Herbs & Plants and *A Kitchen Witch's World of Magical Food.*

Chilli
Chillies Magical Properties: Creativity, energy, power, protection, passion, hex breaking

Coriander
Coriander Magical Properties: Health, healing, peace, love, release, wealth, protection, negativity

Fennel
Fennel Magical Properties: Healing, purification, protection, courage, confidence, fertility, initiation
Mustard
Mustard Magical Properties: Clarity, protection, fertility

Cinnamon
Cinnamon Magical Properties: Success, healing, power, psychic powers, protection, love, focus, lust, spirituality, changes

Rosemary
Rosemary Magical Properties: Protection, love, lust, mental powers, exorcism, purification, healing, sleep

Cakes and drink
Everyone shares cakes and drink.

Closing and thanks to fire
Ness:
>Hestia, Goddess of the Hearth, Home and Keeper of the Sacred Flame.
>We have looked to your virtues of happiness and thank you for your warmth and your blessings.

We have been inspired to be gentle, forgiving and well-centred.

Hail and farewell!

Rachel:

To the great fiery Goddess Pele, powerful reclaimer of land, provider of balance and opportunity who destroys to enable us to restore and renew; the divine mother who reminds us of our own inner greatness, we give thanks to you.

Aloha...the first dawn of light, the spark of the Goddess mother, the symbol of eternity and the gift and blessing of life.

We bid you hail and farewell!

Josh:

Lucifer, God of Light and Spirituality.

You have shown us the fire that burns within us, the light that guides our path.

We thank you for your powers of transformation, so we may find the courage to release ourselves from these chains, ascending to become that which we know ourselves to be.

Hail and farewell!

Tracey:

Wayland of the Spectral Smithy, Wayland of the forest forge, lord of smith craft and forger of the wyrd.

We thank you for your blessings of courage and strength.

Your lessons have transformed and tempered us to withstand all that life may throw at us.

We bid you hail and farewell!

Rachel:

Maiden uncast this circle white; unravel the threads of glowing light.

Mother uncast this circle red, unhook the tightly bound

threads.

Crone uncast this circle black, allow us to keep the knowledge that we lacked.

This circle is open but never broken.

So mote it be!

Kitchen Witch Ritual: Water – Co-Written by Rachel Patterson, Tracey Roberts, Vanessa Armstrong, Joshua Petchey, Sue Perryman and Samantha Leaver

Sam purifies the space and participants using kernips (see the Lustral Water section for more details).

Rachel speaks as the circle is walked by Louisa and Helen, sprinkling rose petals:

> Casting this circle with white, energy woven from the maiden's light.
> Casting this circle red, energy woven from the mother instead.
> Casting this circle black, crone energy woven that we lack.
> This circle is cast may it protect those within and that without.

To call in water, a staff is passed to each person in the circle asking them to state out loud a word that they associate with water, such as rivers, oceans, rain, emotions etc.

Tracey:

> I call to Poseidon, master of the waves and depths whose trident commands the oceans.
> Poseidon, the fury of the cresting breakers, but also the calm in the eye of the storm, bring with you the gifts of patience and determination.
> Help us navigate the changes in our lives; give us the

strength to cruise through the ebb and flow of life's tides. Teach us the magic and mystery of your dark and unfathomable depths.

We invite you into our circle and bid you hail and welcome!

Josh:

I call upon the Orisha Oshun, African Goddess of Water; you are the bearer of prophecy, the bestower of fertility. Your spirited dance, infinite and bewitching, your sweet, soulful song, euphoric and soothing, you enchant our eyes and consume our souls.

Casting your spell of love and peace upon us.

As we taste each raindrop from the sky, may we be cleansed by your healing spirit. As we hear each crash of a river's wave, may we speak with truth and clarity.

Hail and welcome!

Sue:

Hail Aphrodite, Goddess of Love, Beauty, Passion and Desire.

She who was born from the foam of the sea, she who brings forth love in the hearts of Gods and mortals.

Join us if you will in our ritual this day, and bring us your gifts of love and fertility to our rites.

Hail and welcome!

Ness:

I call to Kanaloa, Hawaiian God of the Ocean, bearer of fresh springs – your name means 'great peace and stillness'.

As we bathe in your seas, may our minds be rested and our bodies cleansed, and allow the power of the waters to heal our inner selves.

Hail and welcome!

Introduce the deities

Tracey:

Poseidon is one of the twelve Olympian Gods and brother to Zeus and Hades. These three brothers divided up all of creation between them. Zeus became ruler of the sky, Hades reigned in the Underworld and Poseidon was given dominion over all water, both fresh and salt water.

After dividing the sky, the watery realms and the Underworld, the three Olympian brothers agreed that the Earth itself would be ruled jointly, with Zeus as king. This led to a number of territorial disputes among the Gods. Poseidon vied with Athena to be patron deity of Athens. He demonstrated his power and generosity by striking the Acropolis with his trident, which caused a spring of salt water to emerge. Athena, however, planted an olive tree, which was seen as a more useful favour. And so Athena became the patron deity of Athens and the people built the Parthenon in her honour. But the Athenians were also careful to show honour to Poseidon as well.

Like many Greek Gods, Poseidon can have a bit of a temper and enjoys a dalliance with the ladies, both divine and mortal. His most famous offspring are Helen of Sparta and Theseus, the chap who defeated the Minotaur and Pegasus. Yup the winged horse was Poseidon's work. According to myth, Poseidon took the form of a horse when he seduced Medusa. The result of this union was Medusa being turned into a gorgon by Athena and Pegasus being born out of Medusa's blood when she was decapitated by Perseus.

Poseidon also has a peaceful side, he offers protection to sailors and can provide welcome waters to the land to ensure fertile soil. Working with Poseidon and water energies in general reminds us to stay connected to the deep emotional and instinctual parts of our selves, however uncomfortable, or even painful, it might be.

Josh:

Oshun is the African Yoruba Goddess of Water, Love, Healing, Diplomacy, Order, Prophecy, Dance and Fertility. She is always represented as a beautiful woman and in some cultures she is said to be a mermaid. Whenever Oshun is encountered it is said she is always dancing. One of the main stories of hers speaks of her broken heart. And so she forever dances and sings to soothe her heartache. But she is not a Goddess to be messed with. Her temper is something rarely seen, but when trifled with her calming dancing ceases and the tsunamis and tidal waves begin! Other than this she is loved by all and well known for her healing of the sick. She believes very much in diplomacy, and fighting is not her forté. She was taught by the primordial deities the use of divination using cowry shells. And she passed the knowledge onto us humans making her the Goddess of Prophecy. When invoked, or generally if she is around, her energy will bring a lot of happiness, humour and giggles. Unless of course you are with your significant other then she will give you all the romance, passion and horniness you desire… After all, she is the Goddess of Love and Fertility.

Sue:

Aphrodite is the Greek Goddess of Love, Desire, Passion, Beauty and Procreation. There are two accounts of her birth; one claims that she is the daughter of Zeus and the mother Goddess Dione and the other claims that she arose from the sea foam on a giant scallop shell after Cronus castrated Uranus and threw his genitals into the sea. Aphrodite was married to Hephaestus, the God of Blacksmiths, Sculptures, Metal Work, Fire and Volcanoes, although she had many lovers among both Gods and men. She wears a magical girdle, which makes her irresistible to all men and incites feelings of love and lust wherever she goes. Her Roman equivalent is Venus to whom a famous sculpture is named, the Venus de Milo. She has been the muse of many artists over the centuries including Botticelli in his famous picture The Birth of Venus. She is also associated with the planet Venus. The myrtle tree, dolphins, roses, pomegranates, scallop shells, pearls, doves, sparrows and horses are sacred to her. There are many stories of Aphrodite, including one in which she helped Jason's quest to take the Golden Fleece and another where she is said to have caused the Trojan War.

Ness:

Kanaloa was the Hawaiian God of the Ocean. He was also a healer and a close companion of Kane, who was said to be the God of Creation. Together they would travel, drinking the sacred medicinal drink of Hawaii, 'awa', and using their staves to strike holes in the ground to release clear fresh spring water. Kanaloa would often be symbolised as a squid or octopus. According to some, he caused mischief and was banished to the depths of the oceans, but held on to his power and godhood. Sailors would pray to him to be allowed to cross the watery depths without harm. Likewise he was also worshipped as a God of magic. Kanaloa in Hawaiian is used as a word that means 'seashell'. It also translates to 'the great peace or the great stillness'. According to the Huna Kupua, which is the Hawaiian spirituality principles, Kanaloa represent the core self or the centre of the universe within yourself. If you look into the round eyes of Kanaloa you would see a pattern. This pattern is said to be the Web of Life – the connection of all things to one another. At the centre of this pattern is the spider/shaman or person who is aware of weaving his own path in life. Gazing at this pattern is said to harmonise the physical, mental and emotional energies of yourself.

Rachel:

In many myths and legends life first evolved from the primordial waters. We use this element every day to quench our thirst and to cleanse our bodies. A large proportion of our bodies is made up of this element that is governed by the Moon.

Water is the element of the depths of emotion and of the subconscious. Water rules purification, the unknown, love and all other emotions. Water is associated with absorption and germination and also pleasure, friendship, marriage, fertility, love, happiness, healing, sleep, dreaming, cleansing and psychic acts. Water rules physical things and places such as the womb, the unconscious mind, and any type of water source, from the largest oceans to the morning dew.

The place of water in the ritual circle is in the west, the place of death and transitions. The time of twilight and autumn are associated with water as these are mysterious times. You might find a cup or bowl of water on a witch's altar, but other representations may be a cauldron or shells. Our ancestors saw water as sacred and would give offerings at springs and other natural water sources. We carry on this tradition when we throw coins into fountains and make a wish.

All make herb pouches

Blue fabric pouches are passed around the circle, then various items that correspond to the element of water are added after being charged with intent. Descriptions of the magical properties, myths and history of each herb/spice are read out. Information can be taken from my books *A Kitchen Witch's World of Magical Herbs & Plants* and *A Kitchen Witch's World of Magical Food*.

Camellia

Camellia Magical Properties: Abundance, prosperity, spirituality

Shells

Obviously sea shells are associated with water, the Moon controls the tides of the ocean so shells are also associated with the Moon. Being associated with water and the Moon, the shell works perfectly in spells for emotions too. Shells also have an association with Aphrodite, so can also be used for love spells. Use a shell as a love drawing talisman. In the past shells were also used in some parts of the world as currency so they also have the association of money and prosperity. Think about what a shell is, it is a protective covering for the creature inside making shells also good for protection. Shells can also be used in divination, use in a set with pebbles, crystals and bones to cast a reading (think Tia Dalma in Pirates of the Caribbean).

Cardamom

Cardamom Magical Properties: Love, passion, clarity, uplifting, protection

Lemon Balm

Lemon Balm Magical Properties: Success, healing, anti depression, memory, love, anxiety

Sea glass
I believe sea glass has all the elements of the sea and water wrapped up together, use it as you would sea shells.

Poppy
Poppy Magical Properties: Love, sleep, money, luck, fertility, rebirth, grief

Rose
Rose Magical Properties: Love, psychic powers, healing, luck, protection, peace, mysteries, knowledge, dreams, friendship, death and rebirth, abundance

Cakes and drink
Everyone shares cakes and drink.

Closing and thanks to water
Ness:

Kanaloa, thank you for your presence in this circle today.
Our minds and bodies have been rejuvenated.
As the waves of your waters washed over us, we feel calm and at peace within ourselves.
Hail and farewell!

Sue:

Aphrodite, we thank you for watching over us and bringing your gifts of love and passion to our rites.
Hail and farewell!

Josh:

Goddess of Water, Yoruba Orisha Oshun.
You have brought clarification to our minds, helping us to feel the diplomacy this Earth desires.
We have grasped at your harmonious ambience, and bathed in the bliss of your song.
May we go forth with fluidity of mind and patience of

heart.
Hail and farewell!

Tracey:

Poseidon, master of the waves and the ocean depths. We thank you for the gifts of patience and determination, the strength to cruise through the ebb and flow of life's tides and the light you have shone on our most unfathomable depths.
Hail and farewell!

Rachel:

Maiden uncast this circle white; unravel the threads of glowing light.
Mother uncast this circle red, unhook the tightly bound threads.
Crone uncast this circle black, allow us to keep the knowledge that we lacked.
This circle is open but never broken.
So mote it be.

Author's note: After we held the water ritual we experienced three solid days of torrential rain (it was held in the middle of August, our summer)...be careful with words and what you wish for...

Hellenic Practice

I am very blessed to know a lovely and talented lady who practises the Hellenic pathway and she has shared this Hellenic ritual with me to use in this book so a huge thank you to Samantha Leaver.

Hellenismos aka Dodekatheism, Hellenism, Hellenic Polytheism or Hellenic Reconstructionism is the modern adaptation of the Ancient Hellenic (Greek) religion. Its heart is the worship of the Twelve Olympian Gods – Zeus, Hera, Athena, Hephaistos, Apollon, Artemis, Demeter, Hestia, Hermes, Ares,

Poseidon, and Aphrodite – along with the entire pantheon of the Greek Gods and Goddesses known communally as the Theoi. Most honour other types of divinities, including the various types of nature spirits, Chthonic/Kthonic (Underworld) deities and the heroes, plus spiritual and physical ancestors.

Two types of Hellenismos exist today since its establishment in the 1990s. The Traditional Hellenismos is recreating the practices of the ancients by understanding and applying as much as possible of the fragments of information we have available in the modern-day setting. The other branch is Reformed Hellenismos, which often includes Hellenic Paganism, in other words cherry picking practices that are not strictly Hellenic – including modern-day magic, patron deities and the use of non-Hellenic ritual practices.

There are five steps to a Hellenistic ritual: procession, purification, hymns and prayers, sacrifice/offerings, prayers of supplication and thanks, usually followed by a feast and/or theatre and sporting events.

The procession included carrying everything needed for the ritual, songs and music, weaving its way to the altar, where purification of the participants and the space, using kernips or lustral water, takes place. As part of purification, some sprinkle barley and most toss some into the ritual hearth as a start to the offerings of thanks for requests that are made later. Hymns are sung to invoke the deities and celebrate them, but also to make him or her more inclined to help out. Prayers are the request of the ritual; they are formed with respect and carefully convey the intent of the ritual. The main event is the sacrifice/offering. Modern worship doesn't involve animal sacrifice, but the raw ingredients of the feast to come are often offered, which could include meat. Other things like dried fruit, cake, water, wine libations, seeds, lentils, veggies and blood are used. And finally the thanks, in which – as it sounds – you say thank you to the deities and spirits for their help.

The Hellenic's ritual calendar is mostly based on the Attic calendar of Athens, since it is the one that survives the best, but you will find plenty of variations out there. It is full to bursting with events and rituals throughout the year; some months have ten celebrations or more!

Stenia and Thesmophoria

The Thesmophoria is a fertility festival held in honour of Demeter, Goddess of Agriculture. It mimicked the actions of Demeter as described in the Homeric Hymn to her when she lost her daughter to Hades.

Usually carried out in September, it has similar themes to the autumn equinox with the balance between life and death. The only people allowed to take part in this festival are married women, which is unusual for the Greeks. It was celebrated over three days as far as we know in Athens and has been likened to a three-day women's retreat on a hillside. This was always the best chance women had to escape the home, meet up with other women and taste a bit of independence.

The Stenia is a festival of preparation and purification and happened a few days before the Thesmophoria. Some believe it was this time that Priestesses who had abstained from sex for at least three days before made dough and shaped it into male genitalia, sacrificed piglets and threw them into a chasm on the hill they had been camping out at. These are symbols of fertility.

On the first day of the Thesmophoria, also known as 'anodos' or 'rising up', the women of the town would leave their homes and process to the hills where they would construct crude huts to shelter in and they would sleep on the ground, which must have been really quite uncomfortable.

On the second day, known as 'nesteia' or 'fasting', the women would sit on the ground and fast for the entire day, they would relive the mourning of Demeter who had lost her daughter. They would meditate and channel their strength into the earth for

Demeter who as we know from the myth had stopped tending the earth in her grief.

As their hunger and discomfort grew, they would engage in aiskhrologia – abusive language and crude jokes, they would hurl insults and obscenities at one another, this was because Iambe, a cheeky, wise and sexually free Goddess tried doing this to soothe the mourning Demeter and put a smile on her face.

Nightfall would bring the official beginning of the third day's rites, called the Kaligeneia, meaning 'Fair Offspring'. The evening was ceremony held by torchlight, in memory of how Demeter sought Persephone by Hekate's torches. Some believe that this is the time the Priestesses would retrieve the piglets and dough penises, cover them with grain and put them on the great altar. The other women would clap to scare away the sacred snakes that guarded the chasms and caverns. This 'compost' would be sown the following month, which echoes the role of the cycle of life and death, in order that the earth be fertilised and rejuvenated.

The day time on the third day was full of prayers, thanksgiving and their fast was broken with a great feast. The women would ask for fertility for themselves, their families and crops in the next season and then, with great joy in their hearts, they would return to their homes and their children.

A Modern-Day Ritual for Thesmophoria

The intent of this ritual is to think about the balance of light and dark and the cycles of life and death. Remember you are re-enacting the mourning of Demeter and her search for her daughter, so think about loss, your ancestors, death, as well as the searching and eventually healing and asking for fertility (not necessarily babies) and abundance for the next season.

Personally, I use the calendar available for download from hellion.org to find out when exactly to celebrate, but it feels right in the darker portion of the year, in September, usually after the autumn equinox and before All Hallows.

Tools you will need for any Hellenic style ritual

A bowl of slightly salted water

A white towel

Some bottled water

Offering bowls

Wine (usually red) optionally you could use fruit juice, squash, mead, or just stick with the water

Barley

Hearth fire

Honey cakes (see recipe below)

Matches

Sprig of rosemary (optional)

Incense (optional), frankincense is the traditional one

For Thesomorphia

Pork

Seeds/grains

Salt dough

Your personal thanksgiving and wishes for the season of rebirth on a piece of paper.

Pillar candles/torches (red if possible to represent Hekates' torches)

Insults/the crudest female comedian recording you can find

No sex for at least three days before the ritual

A feast of pork

During the day think about and write down your wishes for the next season, the season of rebirth. Set up your shrine with depictions of Demeter and Persephone and symbols of life/death/light/dark.

Make your salt dough and honey cakes. Recipes follow. Although you probably have your favourite version of salt dough, this one never seems to fail for me.

Salt dough

Ingredients:

1 cup (250 ml) plain flour

1 cup (250 ml) table salt

1 cup (250 ml) boiled water

⅛ (30 ml) cooking oil

Mix flour and salt in a bowl. Make a hole in the centre and pour in boiled water little by little (use a glove to protect your hands or spoon to mix the flour if the water is too hot). Mix the flour, salt and water, add water as necessary until it is not crumbly. Knead the dough for about five minutes until it is smooth. Add the cooking oil to make the dough soft, pliable and smoother. Wrap it in Clingfilm and store in the fridge until you need it. We will shape them during the ritual and then bake them the day after.

Honey cakes

This is a fairly traditional recipe.

Ingredients:

100g (3 ½ oz) flour

50ml (1.7 fl oz) water

2 tablespoons honey

1 tablespoon olive oil

Place the flour in a bowl; add the honey and olive oil and mix. Pour in the water little by little and continue mixing until a dough has formed. Cool this in the fridge for about ten minutes. Tip the ball of dough onto a floured surface and roll out as thinly as possible. Use a pastry cutter to cut the dough and place the rounds on a greased baking tray in a pre-heated oven (200C) for about ten to 15 minutes depending on how thin you have rolled your rounds. Keep an eye on them!

Preparing for the ritual

Eat lightly or not at all on this day, have water or green tea though to keep hydration up. (If you have to eat for medical conditions – EAT; do not put your health at risk).

Prepare a meal to have after the ritual, something using pork would be good, but you want to try to avoid anything that will upset Demeter i.e. seasonal vegetables from her harvest would annoy her. Place some of the raw ingredients on your shrine outside with everything else.

At sunset take a bath and dress in ritual wear. Now most Hellenics will wear white and have a head covering to commune with deity in prayer and ritual. As an eclectic I will probably get shot for this, but I don't always think it is necessary, especially as this kind of ritual is bordering on the Chthonic. I would consider wearing dark colours, although generally I will cover my head with a scarf.

Note: It is best to do this ritual outdoors in a safe place where burying things will not be disturbed or cause a stink.

Approach the altar slowly, perhaps playing some music or drumming. Sit in front of your sacred space and ground and centre as you would normally.

Light the fire as best you can and any incense you have decided to burn, frankincense is traditionally used in Hellenic rituals.

The cleansing/making kernips (lustral water)

Light the sprig of rosemary with a match and extinguish it in your bowl of slightly salted water. If you can't get the rosemary lit, simply extinguish a match in the water and dip the rosemary in.

Say:

May this water be made pure under the eyes of the immortal Gods.

Dip your middle and forefinger of your right hand into the water and cleanse your left hand, do the opposite and if you like place some water on your forehead or third eye to cleanse.
Say:

May this water purify my body.

Dry your hands and forehead with the white towel; you are now ritually pure for ritual.

Casting the circle

Walk a circle or sit and sprinkle the lustral water around your sacred space. Say:

Here is the boundary of this sacred circle.
By the power of the beloved Theoi, the Spirits of Nature, Our ancestors and ourselves, Esto!

The bowl of water is returned to the altar.

Why am I here?

On this night I celebrate Thesomorphia. I am here to share in the mourning of the great Goddess Demeter of Growth and Harvest at her loss of her daughter Persephone, Goddess of Spring and soon to be Queen of the Underworld. I am here to give thanks for what I have reaped, experience death, and ask for fertility/abundance in the season of rebirth.

The scattering

Throw some barley into a sacred hearth fire say:

This hearth will be consecrated as the altar for this rite of Thesomorphia according to Ancient tradition. The holy fire of Hestia comes now from this hearth.

The mixing

Mix the wine/squash/juice and bottled water (not the salted stuff); the glass is held to the sky. Say:

Behold the Waters of Life!

The first libation

Make your first libation – some of the mixture in the cup is poured out on the 'hearth', and then take a sip in offering to Hestia, or touch a drop to your forehead in offering if you can't/don't want to drink. Say:

Hestia, thine is always the first and the last.

The invocations

In a group setting the story of Demeter, Persephone and Hades would be told here. Homer's Hymn to Demeter is lengthy, but worth it and gives us a good idea of where this festival came from. For a solitary ritual, however, we shall evoke her with these words:

I call to Demeter, great lady of the land.
Friend of the farmer, sustainer of mankind.
Daughter of deep hearted Rhea and wily Kronos.
Loving mother of rich-tressed Persephone.
In ancient times you were honoured by country folk above all others.
In all provinces did men and women pray to you and ask your blessing.
Goddess, we see your hand in rows of golden grain

In heavy fruited trees, in fields of scarlet poppies blooming
amongst the barley.
In the passing of seasons.
In the fury of a mother wronged.
Your daughter stolen to the Underworld.
Demeter, mistress of those cherished mysteries and sacred
rites.
By your might and your compassion do we endure.
Do we live our lives.
Demeter, I call to you.

We can also invoke Iambe

I call to Iambe.

Homer called her Iambe.
She is best known as Baubo, the elderly servant of the King of
Eleusis.
Whose bawdy jests roused the grieving Demeter from her
profound depression during her search for her daughter,
Persephone.
And just how did she cheer up the grieving Demeter you ask?
By pulling up her dress and making her laugh at her vagina
and belly.
I call to you Iambe.

The reflection

Light the red pillar candles and reflect upon the loss Demeter
must have felt when her daughter was taken. Remember your
ancestors and the pain of grief, cry if you need to, this is death,
this is darkness. Reflect on any losses you have experienced this
season.

Look to the torches as your guides, visualise the candles
lighting your path and giving you strength. Play the recorded
female comedian, as crude and rude as you find, and have a good

laugh, really belly rumbling laughing. Remember this is your offering to Iambe who helped cheer Demeter up. Feel your strength gaining, filling you from your belly to your heart and visualise pouring that strength into the earth.

Say:

Goddess Demeter, with the help of Iambe I am strong; I am channelling my strength to you from my heart and belly into the depth of the earth.

The sacrifice (spell for fertility/abundance)

Shape the salt dough into male genitalia visualising male vigour. Sprinkle the pork with seeds/grains visualising female strength and fertility. Place these on the altar.

With this representation of fertility and sacred sex I ask the Great Goddess Demeter for...(insert your wishes for abundance and fertility).

Burn your thanksgiving in the hearth fire or off the torches.

With sacred flame I give thanks for...(insert your thanks-givings).

The offering

Go back indoors and bake the salt dough, while baking have your pork feast. Once finished and the salt dough is cooled, take it back outside.

Bury everything in the earth – the seeded pork, the raw ingredients, and the salt dough. Say:

From out of the dark, we look toward the light.
We've made these offerings in the name of abundance might.
Spirits soar high, we feel you near, and these gifts we do bring.
We offer our all, our minds, bodies and souls.

We offer our strength, our spirit set free.
Before you we kneel, the spell we now seal!
This spell that we send is not at an end.
Let the magic we've laid, go forth and not fade!
Houtos Heksoi (So mote it be)!

The final libation

Sip from the cup of wine again or touch to the forehead, extinguish and cool off the hearth with any leftovers. Say:

Hestia, yours always is the first and the last.

The closing

Eat some of the honey cake and then bury the leftovers and the ashes from the hearth alongside everything else. Say:

To all the Gods, we give thanks, for the lessons we have learnt, for the path ahead. In the hope of being blessed with your blessings!

Traditionally Hellenics do not dismiss the deities...but it is a good idea to close the circle and pour the kernips/lustral water into the earth. Say:

May this circle be open, but never broken! Esto!

Protection Ritual by Vanessa Armstrong

You will need

Black candle – this is to dispel negative energies
Black tourmaline crystal – this transmutes into positive energies
Jet – to absorb negative energies
Sage and rosemary bundle to burn as incense for cleansing

Cloves – may be burned for protection and to purify the energy of the area that the ritual is to be held also

Set these items up on your working altar or a small table in the middle of the room.

Circle casting

Standing at your altar, light the candle and incense and say the following:

Here I stand in this sacred space.
Our energies are connected.
By the powers of the elements that reside.
This circle is now protected!

Calling in the quarters

Element of air, I call upon you in this ritual.

Show me positive thinking so that I may banish all negative thoughts.
Teach me the knowledge of freedom so that I may protect myself
Hail and welcome!

Element of fire, I call upon you in this ritual.
Bring with you your fiery force, teaching me to protect what is ours.
Show me your willpower and drive so that I may stand my ground.
Hail and welcome!

Element of water, I call upon you in this ritual.
Bring with you your purification so that I may wash away negative energies.

Teach me intuition so that I may be guided and protected.
Hail and welcome!
Element of earth, I call upon you in this ritual.
Bring with you your focus and your strength so that I can be
guided in my quest for protection.
Show me stability and wisdom so that I may stand my
ground.
Hail and welcome!

You can adjust this, depending on what you need the protection
for. For house protection, sprinkle black salt into each corner of
the home. Smudging with the sage and rosemary bundle into the
corner of each room also has the same effect.

Sit and focus on the lighted candle. Visualise the candle flame
spreading out to protect every room in your house. This can also
be used for self protection too.

If you need protection from a person, write their name on a
piece of paper, light it with the candle flame and place it in a
fireproof dish to burn out. Visualise being protected from that
person as the paper burns away.

Thanking the quarters
Element of earth I thank you for your presence in this circle.

I have focus and strength, stability and wisdom and will work
with these to protect what is mine.
Hail and farewell!

Element of water I thank you for your presence in this circle.
I have washed away all that is negative and am guided by
my intuition to remain protected.
Hail and farewell!

Element of fire I thank you for your presence in this circle.

Your fire is my strength to keep myself and those I love
protected,
and the willpower to stand my ground.
Hail and farewell!

Element of air I thank you for your presence in this circle.
You have shown me positivity and have banished all
negative thoughts.
I now have the knowledge I need to protect myself and my
home.
Hail and farewell!

I have stood in this sacred space.
My energies are connected.
By the powers of the elements that reside.
This circle is undone but still protected!
So mote it be!

Cailleach Ritual by Rachel Patterson and Tracey Roberts

This ritual should ideally be done in a yew tree grove. You also
need some shells and pebbles.

Casting the circle

Walk the circle deosil (clockwise). Say:

Casting this circle with white, energy woven from the
maiden's light.
Casting this circle red, energy woven from the mother
instead.
Casting this circle black, crone energy woven that we lack.
This circle is cast, may it protect those within and that
without.

Calling the quarters and deities

Call in the quarters, going around to each person in turn and letting them say a word that describes the element. Go round the circle first for earth, then air, then fire, then water. Then call in the deities by saying:

> We call upon The Cailleach, wise woman, sage, crone.
> Join us today for our rite.
> Lend us your energies of wisdom and knowledge.
> And help us to release the old and move forward to the new.
> Hail and welcome!

> We call upon Bran the Blessed, warrior God.
> Join us today for our rite.
> Bring us your protection and strength.
> And help guide us among the veils between the worlds.
> Hail and welcome!

Smudge the circle, then give this reading about The Cailleach:

> The Cailleach is the old woman, the crone Goddess who created the mountains by dropping boulders from her apron and then used them as stepping stones. Many parts of the British Isles carry her name and portray her character.
>
> She is the Goddess of the ancestors, of old and age and of winter. Her place in the wheel of the year runs between Samhain and Beltane. She is depicted as being fierce, icy and harsh and her association with the cold freezing weather may have been what led her to sometimes be depicted as blue skinned.
>
> The crone is the grandmother who has gained knowledge and transformed it into wisdom. In many societies she is an elder of the community, is revered and respected and her wise knowledge is sought after by younger members, although we

don't seem to do that so much here, unfortunately. The crone is the Goddess of autumn, the dark months and the Goddess of winter.

Caille is Gaelic for veil. The Cailleach reminds us of all that we hide under our own veils, the veils that we pull across the truth that we hide in our hearts. Sometimes our veils may seem like locked doors that we never intend to open. At other times our veils are drawn to hide something from other people. Veils may be drawn when we are not ready to show our true feelings because the time is not right. We may also need to recognise when others draw a veil, leaving us mystified. Sometimes we must pull veils back to reveal the truth, but there are times when we should respect another's privacy and leave the veil in place.

The Cailleach is also associated with the sea, which is cleansing and purifying. There is an element of danger with the ocean and its power needs to be acknowledged and respected. The shore is a boundary between the realm of water and the realm of earth, between the physical world and the otherworld.

A Cally Berry story

In Ireland there was an old tradition, the first farmer to finish his harvest would make a corn dolly called the Cally Berry or Cailleach, which was also known as the Hag of the Harvest. The farmer would then pass this corn dolly on to the next farmer who finished harvesting and he would pass it on to the next farmer in turn until it ended up with the last farmer to complete his harvest. This slowest farmer would then be obliged to look after the Cailleach for the entire winter until the start of the next sowing season.

This was considered very unfortunate in some respects as the corn dolly Cailleach was said to have a huge appetite and was thought to eat out of house and home the farmer who was looking after her. However, the farmer could also not dispose of the corn dolly as doing so would blight his crops if he slighted her in such a manner.

There was an upside to looking after the Hag of the Harvest though, as the farmer could hang it on his plough horse for good luck on the first day of ploughing the next spring, so if the farmer could provide hospitality for the Cailleach all winter he would be rewarded with an extra bountiful harvest the next year.

Working

The HPS:

> We are going to work together with the symbolism of the yew tree as we have the grove here, the death and rebirth energy of the Cailleach and the association of the cleansing and purifying sea with the shells and pebbles as symbols.
>
> Anyone who wishes to walk through may, but there is no pressure if you choose not to.
>
> We will start by stating our purpose:
>
> This ritual is to leave behind guilt, let go of the negative thought patterns and restore integrity and positive energy. So mote it be!
>
> Within the yew tree grove walk a circle, pick up a stone from the centre and walk out of the yew tree grove and round to the field – throw the stone out as far as you can letting it take the negative energy with it then walk back into the yew tree grove – collect a pretty shell or pebble and instil it will positive energy to take home with you.

After the ritual, everyone feasts, then spends some time remembering the ancestors.

The HPS:

All join hands and say out loud or remember those that have passed before us and those that we honour at this time of the year and always.

Closing

To Bran the Blessed we give our thanks for joining us today, may we take comfort from your strength in the future.
Hail and farewell.

To The Cailleach we give our thanks for your wisdom and knowledge and the support we can take away with us today.
Hail and farewell.

We thank the elements of earth, air, fire and water for lending your energies to this rite today, may we always be blessed with your presence.
Hail and farewell.

Walk the circle widdershins.

The HPS:

Maiden uncast this circle white, unravel the threads of glowing light.
Mother uncast this circle red, unhook the tightly bound threads.
Crone uncast this circle black, allow us to keep the knowledge that we lacked.
This circle is open but never broken.
So mote it be.

The Art of Ritual

Elen Ritual by Rachel Patterson and Tracey Roberts

Casting the circle

The HPS walks the circle with an antler and says:

Casting this circle with white, energy woven from the maiden's light.
Casting this circle red, energy woven from the mother instead.
Casting this circle black, crone energy woven that we lack.
This circle is cast may it protect those within and that without.

Calling the quarters and deities

Everyone calls in the quarters. Going around to each person in turn they say a word that describes the element. Go round the circle first for earth, then air, then fire then water.
Smudge the circle, they call in the deities by saying:

Elen of the Ways, light of the land, on you we call.
Brighten up our souls in these golden days of autumn.
Goddess of the forest and all creatures who dwell within.
Grant us illumination and courage, grace and wisdom.
By all the powers of autumn and the sacred spring.
Energy and transformation we ask you to bring to this rite .
We bid you hail and welcome!

Herne the Hunter, Lord of the Wild Hunt, on you we call.
Be the fire within our hearts in these golden days of autumn.
God of the forest and all things wild and free.
Grant us protection and stamina, patience and understanding.
By all the powers of autumn and the changing of the trees.
We bid you hail and welcome!

Reading

Elen is an ancient British Goddess, and when I say ancient I

210

mean Palaeolithic, a time when reindeer roamed in this country. Elen is a mysterious and elusive deity, but she has many connections.

She appears in that Welsh myth (Mabinogion) as a shamanic sort of deity. The emperor of Rome dreams of her sitting on a golden throne and becomes determined to find her. This Elen is a Goddess of precognitive dreams and soul journeys. In time or maybe an echo of her past, she became associated with the land and all of its roads, paths, ley lines and trackways. This is her aspect of Elen of the Ways and the first Roman highways were thought to have been invented by her. There are also several wells and waterfalls in Britain that are thought to be sacred to Elen, in time some of these became Christianised as St Helen's Wells

Her name is believed to mean light or light bearer, giving Elen another layer as a Goddess of fire, as well as water and earth. With fire being the magical element of transformation Elen is always changing and transforming.

As we see the seasons change and the animals start to migrate; you can feel her presence in the energies that flow through the Earth and it is that energy that we can work with during the Mabon season. In the spring Elen appears as a maiden cloaked in green, with an antlered headdress, or she can be a lady of fire in the autumn months. It is this aspect that we will be working with today, so picture her now as a beautiful woman with long red hair and a scarlet gown with golden leaves. She will bring you warmth, enlightenment and magic into these glorious autumn days.

Working

Everyone joins in a spiral dance, ending with being led between two candles – one to burn away negativity and one to bring in positive energy, bringing in balance.

After this there is feasting.

Thank deity

Herne the Hunter, Lord of the Wild Hunt.
God of the forest and all things wild and free.
We thank you for joining us in our rite today.
Farewell and blessed be!

Elen of the Ways, light of the land.
Goddess of the forest and all creatures who dwell within.
We thank you for joining us in our rite today.
Farewell and blessed be!

Releasing the quarters and uncasting the circle

Spirits of the four quarters, we thank you for joining our ritual here today, you are free to return to your time and space with love and blessings.
Hail and farewell!

The HPS walks the circle widdershins and says:

Maiden uncast your circle white, release your threads of glowing light.
Mother uncast your circle red, release the strands of energy led.
Old Crone, uncast your circle black, we thank you for the knowledge that we lacked.
By the elements of earth, air, fire and water.
This circle is open but never broken.
So mote it be!

Sulis Ritual by Rachel Patterson and Tracey Roberts

Casting the circle

The HPS sprinkles marigold petals while walking deosil around the circle. She says:

Casting this circle with white, energy woven from the maiden's light.
Casting this circle red, energy woven from the mother instead.
Casting this circle black, crone energy woven that we lack.
This circle is cast may it protect those within and that without.

Call the quarters

We call to the guardians of the south and the element of fire, come join us in our circle.
Bring your warmth, passion and energy.
Hail and welcome!

We call to the guardians of the west and the element of water, come join us in our circle.
Bring your cleansing waves of emotion.
Hail and welcome!

We call to the guardians of the north and the element of earth, come join us in our circle.
Bring your stability and grounding.
Hail and welcome!

We call to the guardians of the east and the element of air, come join us in our circle.
Bring your intuition and intellect.
Hail and welcome!

Calling deity

Sulis, Lady of the Sacred Wells, we call to you.
Goddess of the healing Sun and thermal springs.
Cleanse our hearts and clear our minds.
We invite you to join our circle and ask for your blessings.

Hail and welcome!!

Lord of the Sun, light of day, we call to you.
And in your ancient names we celebrate.
We invite you to join our circle and ask for your blessings.
Hail and welcome!!

Reading about Sulis

Mention the Goddess Sulis and you immediately think of Aqua Sulis in Bath. These thermal springs have been in use for 10,000 years, so when the Celts arrived on our shores they probably found Sulis already ruling there and they more than likely went with that and built their own shrines in her honour.

We know that Sulis is a Goddess of healing waters, but she is so much more. We have forgotten that she was originally worshipped as a solar and fertility deity. Her name is derived from the word Sun or Sol and she was served by Priestesses who kept her eternal flame burning. The perpetual fires and hot springs remind us of her origins. Sulis's power reflects the divine light of the Sun filtered through the healing power of water, helping Her human children and their plants to grow and prosper. (From Judith Shaw's Blog)

Sulis will grant you healing, blessings and curses to those who pray and give offerings at her shrine. Yep curses. Many requests for curses have been found written on lead tablets at the shrines of Sulis. The curses were usually made in connection with something that had been stolen and the person would be released from the curse when they returned what they had taken.

Working

A large bowl is placed in the centre of the circle and everyone is handed a small silver coin. The coins are charged with intent and wishes and then thrown into the bowl of water with a petition to Sulis. These coins will then be taken to city of Bath (Somerset) and dropped into the waters of Sulis.

Healing work can be done by holding hands, raising energy and sending a little out to those who need it.

This is followed by feasting and then a talking stick is passed around to each person so that they can give thanks and blessings.

Closing

Lord of the Sun, light of day.
In your fire boat gliding through golden rays.
We thank you for your warmth and blessings.
Stay if you will, go if you must.
We bid you hail and farewell!

Sulis, Lady of the Sacred Wells.
Goddess of the healing Sun and thermal springs.
We thank you for cleansing our hearts and granting our wishes.
Stay if you will, go if you must.
We bid you hail and farewell!

Release the quarters

Guardians of the east, element of air,
Return in peace to your mighty realm
We bid you hail and farewell!

Guardians of the north, element of earth,
Return in peace to your mighty realm
We bid you hail and farewell!

Guardians of the west, element of water,
Return in peace to your mighty realm
We bid you hail and farewell!

Guardians of the south, element of fire,
Return in peace to your mighty realm
We bid you hail and farewell!

Uncasting the circle
Walk the circle widdershins, then say:

Maiden uncast your circle white, release your threads of glowing light.
Mother uncast your circle red, release the strands of energy led.
Old Crone, uncast your circle black, we thank you for the knowledge that we lacked.
By the elements of earth, air, fire and water.
This circle is open but never broken.
So mote it be!

Summary and Random Thoughts

These are the basics of a ritual; there are so many variations possible, and how formal you want it to be or not is up to you. Nothing is right or wrong because it is your ritual and don't let anyone tell you otherwise.

A circle can be cast for no reason other than to sit in silence and contemplate your naval, a ritual can be performed for no point other than to practise your ritual skills or for any reason that you want, make it yours.

All of the rituals here, the workings, quarter calls, chants and circle castings are to the best of our knowledge and memories original to us, but the mind can play tricks and ultimately there are only so many ways and words you can use to call in an element. If we have unknowingly borrowed a sentence or two from somewhere it was done so with respect and brains like sieves...

I have been in many circles and each one has been different depending on what group is running it, who wrote it, how it was written, what tradition the group is and ultimately who is in the circle. The energy in a ritual is made up from the combined energies of those that are there.

Make it so...

Moon Books invites you to begin or deepen your encounter with Paganism, in all its rich, creative, flourishing forms.